3080
3080
82

Southern Electric Album

Alan Williams

LONDON

IAN ALLAN LTD

First published 1977

ISBN 0 7110 0806 X

Published by Ian Allan Ltd, Shepperton, Surrey, and printed in the United Kingdom by Crampton & Sons Ltd, Sawston, Cambridge.

Cover: Hurrying through the countryside near Polhill on May 30 1973 comes 4CEP No 7184 at the head of a 12-car CEP/BEP/CEP formation on a Charing Cross-Dover working. */J. H. Cooper-Smith*

Front endpaper: Brake and shoegear rattling distinctively, 2BIL 2032 brakes for the speed restriction through Clapham Junction with the 12.57 Waterloo-Alton/Portsmouth train on 14 March 1952. */R. E. Vincent*

Title page: Winding uphill into the gloom of Portsmouth and Southsea High Level station comes 4BUF 3080 at the head of the 14.50 Waterloo-Portsmouth Harbour on 29 July 1970. */J. Scrace*

Below: Disturbing the tranquility of rural Sussex in Summer 1972 is a 4BEP at the head of a Victoria-Brighton train crossing the elegant but troublesome Ouse Valley Viaduct. */P. A. Dolson*

Introduction

'Juicer', 'flashbox', 'spark', emu—call them what you will, Southern electrics have transformed the face of Southern England while becoming part of it. Transformed it, because they have brought scores of towns in Kent, Sussex, Surrey and Hampshire within commuting distance of London. Part of it because, thanks to electrification, even in these post-Beeching days, you don't have to go very far in Southern England before you stumble across a railway station. And chances are, whatever the time of day, and despite the latest round of economies, you'll not have long to wait for a train.

It is over 60 years now since the first suburban lines were electrified, and 40 since the tentacles of conductor rail crept outwards from the suburban network down to the sea at Brighton, Worthing, Eastbourne, Hastings, Bognor and Portsmouth. Since the War, electrification has spread further east into all of Kent, and westwards as far as Bournemouth, so that nowadays the vast majority of the lines which comprise the Southern Region are electrified, all on the same outside third conductor-rail system.

Development of rolling stock for this vast system very closely followed the geographical expansion of electrification, each new scheme bringing a requirement for new stock, or further batches of existing designs, and this Album is therefore uniquely able to trace at the same time both the historical development of the Southern Electric system and its rolling stock, from the first suburban schemes of the Edwardian era to the present-day replacement stock.

It is doubtful if, when in 1913 the Directors of the London & South Western Railway decided to electrify their company's Thames Valley suburban lines to placate mounting public dissatisfaction with their existing services, many realised that they were taking the first steps towards the creation of what is still the world's greatest and busiest urban electric railway system. But their newly-appointed and farsighted General Manager, Herbert Walker, may well have perceived the possibilities; certainly it was he who, when the Southern Railway was formed in 1923, took the initiative to forestall the SECR's plans for a 1500V third and fourth-rail scheme, and to curtail development of the Brighton's overhead system, so that less than a decade later the Southern could boast a totally electrified suburban railway, equipped entirely on the ex-LSWR 600V third rail system.

Arguments as to the wisdom of Walker's choice have raged back and forth ever since, fuelled anew each time the Southern's conductor rails fall prey to the peculiarly disruptive freezing rain of Southern England—and the train service falls apart as a result! Certainly the Brighton's overhead system, though clumsy, intrusive and complicated in suburban areas, was technically superior, especially for the later main line schemes. But, as more recent experience has shown, overhead electrification is hideously expensive, and it is doubtful whether even such a practical man as Walker could have justified many of his schemes on this basis.

Walker had a strong awareness of his shareholders' interests and successive schemes were carefully planned to bring the maximum advantages of electrification with the minimum of outlay on track and signalling. Not for Walker were the 'new railway' concepts of today and as a result, even now, despite the relatively high levels of traffic, many of the outlying areas of the system remain semaphore signalled, with neat but Victorian stations and block controls dating back to the beginning of the Century.

Some will say that the Southern's problem was simply that the system got too big too quickly; and it is certainly true that the rapid series of suburban and, later, main line extensions in the 1920s and 1930s precluded the provision of all-new stock, and that the Southern was obliged to resort to rebuilding displaced steam stock for some services. But its Board could hardly have foreseen the rigours, intensity and duration of the Second World War, or the uncertainties of its aftermath, leading up to Nationalisation in 1948, with its new criteria and competition for funds from the rather less well developed railways north of the Thames! Walker was a realist; had he opted for the technically superior but vastly more expensive overhead system, or insisted on modernising the infrastructure as well, most of the schemes would simply never have got off the ground.

Throughout its history, perhaps influenced

1206
H

by its thrifty LSWR and LBSCR predecessors, and certainly by Walker, the Southern practised careful husbandry in the construction and use of rolling stock; as explained in the following pages, coach bodies, underframes, bogies, even buffers, were all re-used until life-expired, and it was no coincidence that Eastleigh was still building vehicles to SR design on recovered underframes in 1960, 12 years after Nationalisation. But regrettably, the Southern Electric paid dearly for its careful planning; because it was electrified and therefore, by definition, relatively modern, apart from the Kent Coast extensions much of the 1955 Modernisation Plan passed it by. Moreover, its commitment to the use of salvaged underframes and standardised equipment for the majority of its suburban stock dictated the adoption of conventional designs and precluded for a further generation any attempts at such radical and much-needed improvements as air-operated doors, fully-automatic couplers, through gangways or air conditioning.

The Southern, quite simply, lost the initiative in the 1950s and 1960s, producing some decidedly mediocre stock, both suburban and main line. But it now stands poised at the threshold of replacement of its now sadly-outdated suburban fleet and the 4PEP prototypes are the most promising development for many years.

Among enthusiasts, the Southern, and particularly the Southern Electric, has for decades suffered an unwarranted reputation for drab, uninteresting uniformity. Yet, as the following pages reveal, there are now more major types of electric locomotive and multiple-unit working on the Southern alone than there are diesel locomotive types at work throughout the country.

The Southern Electric in its heyday; shortly after the completion of the Reading line electrification in 1939, three trains depart from Guildford simultaneously, all bound for Waterloo but via different routes. On the left, one of the original LSWR 'nutcracker' sets, now 3SUB No 1206, leads a Cobham line train out of the bay, while in the centre of the scene 4COR 3121 and a 4RES on a Portsmouth Harbour-Waterloo fast pace 2BIL 2087 leaving on a Waterloo via Aldershot and Ascot working. /*SR*

The LBSCR was the first of the Southern lines to feel the effect of competition from the newly-electrified LCC tramways on its inner suburban services—traffic on the South London line between Victoria and London Bridge dropped by half between 1902 and 1909.
As early as 1903 the LBSCR had obtained Parliamentary powers to electrify its entire system—mainly to head off proposals for an entirely new high-speed electric line from London to Brighton—and from the outset, therefore, it sought a system that would be suitable for both suburban and main-line traffic. By early 1906 it had decided to adopt a 6,700V ac overhead system—ironically, in view of subsequent developments, because it was felt to be more suited to main-line use than a direct current system with conductor rails. Contracts were let to AEG of Berlin for the design of the overhead equipment and because of its spectacular loss of traffic, the 8½mile South London line was clearly the first priority.
Trial trains began running in January 1909, and public services began on December 1; to work the new services, eight three-car trains were provided, consisting of a first-class side-corridor trailer between two motor brake thirds with all axles powered. For their time, they were both of generous proportions and appointment, being markedly superior to most contemporary LBSCR suburban stock. However, it soon became obvious that, in addition to having too many first-class compartments, the three-car sets provided too much accommodation in slack hours, but not nearly enough during the morning and evening peaks. So from 1910 to 1912, the eight first-class trailers were withdrawn, equipped for steam working and put to work on main-line services, whilst each motor coach was equipped with a driving trailer composite converted from suburban steam stock, making 16 two-car units which could be used singly in slack hours, but in multiples of two or three during the peak. They remained in this form until the abandonment of ac working on the South London line in June 1928; a single two-car unit on a Victoria-bound train enters the old South Bermondsey station *(below)* in the final months of ac working. Note the 'SL' (South London) headcode and the conductor rails already in position in readiness for dc working.
In the first year of electric working, passenger carryings on the 'Elevated Electric' practically doubled, bringing traffic almost back to the halcyon pre-tramway days. It was not surprising, therefore, that the directors of the LBSCR soon resolved to press ahead with further extensions. Early in 1910 the District Railway was making noises about extending its line from Wimbledon to Sutton, and the LBSCR responded with a show of strength by towing a South London unit down for clearance tests. But no more came of the proposals, and the Brighton turned its attention to electrification of the lines from London Bridge and Victoria to Crystal Palace, Norwood Junction and a new depot at Selhurst. For these services, which came into operation from Victoria in May 1911 and from London Bridge in March 1912, 30 three-car sets were provided. Because of the restricted loading gauge through Crystal Palace tunnel, the rolling stock for these services was narrower than the South London line vehicles and was of orthodox compartment layout. Unusually, all three vehicles in each set included a driver's compartment, allowing some flexibility in marshalling; the Crystal Palace train at Victoria *(below right)* is formed of a five car set including two motor coaches. Like all Brighton ac stock, these sets sported externally-illuminated headcode panels and the curious mechanically-operated head/tail disc.
Encouraged by the success of the South London and Crystal Palace schemes, the LBSCR decided in 1913 to electrify most of its remaining suburban lines, and work on the extensions was well in hand when, with the outbreak of War in 1914, the supply of equipment from the German makers was abruptly cut off and all work stopped.
Because of post-war uncertainty and the disruption of supplies, work did not recommence until 1922, and by the time the extensions from Balham to Coulsdon and Sutton were opened on 1 April, 1925, the Southern Railway had practically decided in principle to standardise on the LSWR's low voltage dc third-rail system. As a result, the new stock provided for these services had a brief life of little over four years in their ac form; by September 1929 all the ac lines had been converted to third rail operation.
As built, the stock consisted of 20 five-car units, formed of two driving trailer thirds, a driving trailer composite and a composite marshalled on either side of a motor van,

which, complete with driving compartments, was to all intents and purposes an electric locomotive *(above)*. The reasoning behind this departure from earlier practice and the adoption of the motor van principle remains obscure—they were never used as 'locomotives'—but certainly it was not popular with passengers, who found a full-length non-passenger coach in the centre of the train inconvenient. Clearly the Southern came to think likewise, because whereas most of the ac stock was withdrawn in 1928-1929, stripped and converted to dc operation and returned to traffic as 3SUB units, the motor vans—known to the staff as 'milk vans'—languished in Streatham Hill sidings for some years until finally converted to bogie goods brake vans. */H. C. Casserley, Ian Allan Collection*

Although the LSWR, like its neighbour the 'Brighton', began to feel the effects of rival means of transport on its suburban services from 1900 onwards, it was rather slower to take action, even though the competition, in the form of the District Railway and Central London and Piccadilly tubes, as well as the London United Tramways, was even more severe, especially in the Thames Valley. Indeed, it was not until 1913, after much public agitation for improved services and an approach by dissatisfied local authorities to the Central London to ask that it should extend its proposed Richmond line into the Thames Valley, that the newly appointed General Manager Herbert Walker announced the Company's intention to undertake a comprehensive electrification scheme covering the lines from Waterloo to Wimbledon via East Putney (part of which, from Putney to Wimbledon, was already traversed by the District's electric trains); the Kingston and Hounslow loops, and the Shepperton and Hampton Court branches. At a later date, all three routes to Guildford, via Woking, Cobham and Epsom, would be included. Acting on the advice of both its own electrical engineer and its Consulting Engineers, the LSWR decided to adopt the 600V dc third rail system, with running rail return. As if to make amends for its earlier tardiness, the LSWR swung into action with remarkable speed; although progress was inevitably delayed by the outbreak of War, construction work was able to continue, and the first electric trains began to run between Waterloo and Wimbledon via East Putney in October 1915, followed by the Kingston and Shepperton lines in January 1916, the Hounslow loop in March and the Hampton Court line in June. To work these new services, the LSWR provided 84 three-coach units, Nos E1-E84, converted at Eastleigh from steam-hauled suburban stock. Each was formed of two driving motor coaches, with a trailer sandwiched between; unlike the flat-fronted 'Brighton' ac units, they had rather stylish panelled 'torpedo' pointed front ends, on which were mounted the jumper cables for multiple working, as seen *(right)* during coupling operations soon after the introduction of electric working at Durnsford Road. Because the opal glass headcode panels were not ready, some units were delivered with the aperture temporarily sheeted over, as on unit E12 *(below)* as it poses for a publicity shot in the Putney line bays at Wimbledon during trials; the tail-lamp to the left of the buffer beam gives the game away—the picture is taken from the buffer stop end and if the driver were to heed the guard's green flag he would accelerate smartly across the concourse! Note the fourth rail for District Railway trains and sister Unit E11 in the short bay at the far end of the platform.

The driving cabs of these 'Nutcracker' sets—so called because of the sharp clicking of their electrical equipment—were austere but capacious *(left)*. Instruments were few, being restricted to the brake gauges and an Ammeter. The small button above the master controller admitted air to the whistle, while the lever alongside activated the windscreen wiper, also air-operated. Under the SR, the LSWR units became 3SUB Nos 1201-1284, and from 1934 they were all rebuilt with two additional compartments per coach and mounted on standard SR underframes. After the Second World War they were given an additional trailer from withdrawn trailer sets, redesignated 4SUB and renumbered in the 4131-71, 4195-4234 series. It is in this form that No 4143 is seen *(below left)* at Richmond just after Nationalisation on an up Kingston 'roundabout'. */Metro-Vick, SR*

Faced with the need for additional electric stock for both the 1925 Eastern Section electrification and the Western Section extensions to Dorking and Guildford, the Southern decided it could not possibly withdraw and convert sufficient existing steam suburban vehicles without causing a severe shortage of rolling stock, so 55 completely new three-coach units were ordered. Clearly the LSWR method of electrification had found favour with the Southern Railway Board, for the first 26 units, intended for the Western Section extension and numbered 1285-1310, were modelled on the LSWR units and even had the same 'torpedo' front ends. With its flush steel-panelled sides intricately lined to represent raised wooden panelling, motor coach 8149 of unit 1296 looks resplendent *(top)* outside the Saltley works of its builder, Metropolitan CW&F Co. The Eastern Section units, Nos 1496-1524, were of similar construction, but had an additional compartment in each coach, and a flatter, only slightly bowed front end. Unit 1504 is pacing T9 4-4-0 No E726 *(above)* as it passes Bromley on an Orpington working on 1 August 1932.

Both the Western and Eastern section units were originally

fitted with 'MCB' automatic couplers between coaches within the unit, but after a series of breakaways caused by coupling failures, they were removed and replaced with orthodox semi-permanent three-link couplings. With their 300hp motors, the '1925' stock could be relied upon to give a good turn of speed—especially on the new Guildford via Cobham service, with its 12 mile non-stop dash down the Western Section main line to Surbiton. As electrification progressed over the next few years, and the Eastern, Central and Western Sections became electrically linked, so the suburban stock became more and more 'common user', and the 1925 units were no exception, both types running on all three sections. Like all the other 3SUB units, the 1925 units were augmented to 4SUB after the Second World War. They each received a new all-steel trailer and the Western Section Units became Nos 4301-25; unit 4308 is seen *(above)* at Crystal Palace in the late 50s on an off-peak Victoria-Beckenham Junction working. */Locomotive Publishing Co (2); R. C. Riley*

The Eastern Section 1925 units were renumbered 4326-54 on augmentation. Unit No 4348 restarts from Tulse Hill *(above)* on a Holborn Viaduct-Wimbledon-Sutton working in the late 50s, while in the right distance a post-War all-steel 4SUB approaches on the line from London Bridge. The 1925 stock survived in traffic longer than any other type of unit, not being withdrawn until 1959-61. Even then, they were not all broken up; 10 pairs of Eastern Section motor coaches were modified and returned to traffic as two coach motor de-icing units Nos S92-S101 and survive today, now more than 50 years old, as Departmental Units 011-20. Although they have been stripped internally, apart from the fitting of side periscopes, rail-spraying shoes to the non-motored bogies and roller blind indicators, they remain externally very much in original condition. Unit 019 was stabled for the summer when photographed at Wimbledon in April 1973, alongside 4PEP 4002 *(below)*, but in winter the units are based at Fratton, Brighton, Selhurst, Gillingham and Wimbledon Park. The comparison in front end design, spanning almost 50 years, is revealing. */R. C. Riley; R. E. Ruffell*

The Eastern Section 1925 units proved to be the prototypes for all further new suburban stock right up to the Second World War, although all subsequent units were rebuilt from displaced pre-Grouping suburban steam stock rendered redundant by electrification rather than built new. For the 1925 and 1926 Eastern Section schemes, 105 new three-car units, Nos 1401-95, 1525-34 were provided, rebuilt at Ashford and Brighton on standard SR underframes from SECR four- and six-wheelers. They had the same slightly bowed front end as the '1925' units, the same electrical equipment, and until they suffered similar troubles, 'MCB' automatic couplers, but retained all their characteristic SECR fittings. Thirty further units, Nos 1601-30, were built in 1928 for the Central Section electrification schemes; unit 1421 *(above)* hurries down the through line at Honor Oak Park on a Charing Cross-Tattenham Corner working in August 1933, while *(below)* a sister unit, by now 4SUB No 4464 with an all-steel post-War trailer, runs into Clapham Junction on a Waterloo-Shepperton working on 8 November 1949. */Locomotive Publishing Co; C. C. B. Herbert*

2

The stock provided for the 1928 Central Section electrification schemes included the first dc units rebuilt from LBSCR stock—Nos 1631-57, converted from steam-hauled seven-coach bogie block trains. Ironically, some of this stock, displaced by the 1925 overhead ac extensions four years earlier, was now itself displacing the ac stock as these services were converted to dc operation. On a snowy day in February 1946, 3SUB Unit No 1635 restarts from Elmstead Woods *(above left)* on a Sevenoaks train.
As the ac services were gradually converted to dc operation, the original stock was taken out of service, stripped and sent to works for conversion to dc units. Of units Nos 1702-72 introduced between 1928 and 1930, all but 1701-16 and 1770/1 were converted from ac stock; the remainder, like the earlier batch, were converted from steam stock. All had the characteristic low roof profile of 'Brighton' stock, and most retained their original fittings. Most units received 'augmentation' all-steel trailers after the war and became 4SUBs numbered in the 4517-94 series.
Also rendered redundant by the demise of ac overhead working were the original South London line motor coaches dating from 1909; their driving trailers (see page 8) were included in the general rebuilding scheme, but the side-gangway motor cars were too wide overall for general service. From 17 June, 1928, when dc working replaced ac trains on the South London line, the service was provided by new 3SUB units while the 16 motor coaches were stripped and rebuilt as eight 2SUB units, Nos 1901-08, half the motor coaches becoming driving trailer composites. They returned to traffic on the South London line just under a year later, in May 1929, and were the first units to carry numerical rather than letter headcodes. Although extensively modified, all eight units retained the flattened roof section over the guard's compartment which had previously carried the overhead collectors, and this remained a distinctive feature until their withdrawal in 1954.
Meanwhile, in readiness for the electrification of the single track Wimbledon-West Croydon branch in 1930, four more units of generally similar design, Nos 1909-12, were built in 1929, using the bodies of the original South London line ac unit first-class trailers, which had for some time been in use as locomotive-hauled stock. Like the first eight units, they were 9ft 6in wide overall and were restricted to the section for which they were built, and the South London line, over which they occasionally worked when that section was short of stock. In April 1934 all 12 units were renumbered 1801-12; two of the South London line units are entering London Bridge *(above)* on a rush-hour working from Victoria towards the end of their working life in the early 1950s, while one of the later units, No 1810, sets off *(left)* along the single line from Mitcham Junction towards Beddington Lane on the 11.32 Wimbledon-West Croydon working on 23 October 1954, not many weeks before its withdrawal. Note the unique full-width letter-style numerical headcode used on this route. */SR; R. C. Riley; J. J. Smith*

In the mid-1950s, the 'Brighton' 4SUBs were reformed again, losing their all-steel compartment trailers to new 4EPB units and gaining instead additional LBSCR trailers from condemned units. Renumbered at the same time into a new 45XX series, the new units looked much neater; No 4515 swings away from Peckham Rye *(above)* on a Sevenoaks-Holborn Viaduct via Catford working in the late 50s. Exceptionally, unit 4501 of this new series, seen *(below)* leaving Hampton Court for Waterloo, was only half 'Brighton'—one motor coach and trailer were from an ex-LSWR unit. In addition to the conversions from ex-SECR and LBSCR stock, two batches of units, Nos 1658-1701 and 1773-85, were rebuilt between 1928 and 1930 from LSWR bogie block sets; unlike the original LSWR units of 1915, however, they had the slightly bowed front end of their contemporaries, and were mounted on standard length SR underframes. Early in 1931, 11 more units, Nos 1786-96 appeared, formed from the bodies of two LSWR six-wheelers mounted together on a single underframe. The final conversions of steam stock were two small batches converted from LSWR stock at Eastleigh in 1934/5 (Nos 1585-99) and 1937 (Nos 1579-84). The former had $7\frac{1}{2}$-compartment motor coaches and, like all previous units, all-electric control gear mounted above the underframe in a small compartment behind the driver; the latter, however, had eight-compartment motors and were the first to have electro-pneumatic control gear mounted below the underframe.

Like all the other 3SUBs, these units were augmented to four-car units after the War, reclassified 4SUB and renumbered. Some, like the original LSWR units, were given additional LSWR trailers and renumbered 4172-94 and 4235-50; unit 4235 is approaching Clapham Junction *(above)* with a Victoria-Epsom train on 12 November 1949. Others acquired new all-steel trailers and were renumbered 4401-31 (the six electro-pneumatic units became 4424-9) and 4517-94. One of these units, the erstwhile 3SUB No 1782, became 4SUB 4579; when it was withdrawn in July 1953, it lost its all-steel trailer to a new 4EPB unit, but the remaining three cars, instead of being withdrawn, were stripped and fitted internally as a mobile classroom, reappearing in April 1956 as Departmental unit S10. It was renumbered 053 in 1971 and is seen *(below)* at Fratton on 27 September of that year, still externally virtually in mint condition. It was finally withdrawn in 1974, when it was replaced by a converted all-steel 4SUB unit, but hopes that it might be preserved appear to have been frustrated. */R. C. Riley; G. M. Kichenside; C. C. B. Herbert; J. Scrace*

The only non-suburban units to be rebuilt from steam stock rather than constructed new were the 2NOL units, Nos 1813-90, converted from LSWR main line non-corridor stock at Eastleigh from 1934-36. The motor coaches had $7\frac{1}{2}$ third-class compartments, while the driving trailers had three first- and six third-class compartments; Nos 1813-27 were provided for Brighton-West Worthing stopping services, while Nos 1828-62 were converted in 1935 for the Horsted Keynes-Seaford and Brighton-Seaford, Eastbourne and Hastings stopping services. Unit 1824, together with a sister, pauses *(above)* at Hastings in June 1958, less than a year before it was withdrawn.

The final batch of NOLs, Nos 1863-90, were converted in 1936 for use on the Waterloo-Windsor and Weybridge services and the last eight, Nos 1883-90, had electro-pneumatic control gear; unit 1886 heads an up Weybridge/Windsor train past North Sheen *(below)* on 8 November 1949, by which time the Windsor line units had, like all suburban area stock, become third class only. The NOLs suffered considerable war damage, and several motor coaches went to blitzed 4SUB units. Unit 1853 was involved in the disastrous accident and fire at Barnes in December 1955; the driving trailer was completely destroyed and the motor coach broken up on the spot. Withdrawal began in 1956; most of the London area units had gone by the end of the following year, their underframes being used for SR 2HAP units 5601-36, but many of the Coast units survived until early 1959 (although paradoxically by then mainly working on suburban services), when they too were withdrawn and their underframes used for SR 2EPB units 5651-84.
/B. K. B. Green; C. C. B. Herbert

BOAC
BOAC
BOAC
2923
14

For the Southern's first main-line electrification scheme, to Reigate, Brighton and Worthing, 40 four-car semi-fast units were ordered. Introduced early in 1932, these 4LAV units were basically glorified suburban units with three compartment coaches and only one composite trailer with a side corridor and lavatories. Because of the worsening economic situation of the period, the original intention to provide both fast and slow services to Worthing as well as Brighton did not materialise and the last seven units were cancelled, their underframes and electrical equipment, which had already been supplied, being used instead for subsequent 3SUB conversions. The LAVs were notable as being the first units to be fitted with periscopes for the guard instead of the time-honoured side duckets. Originally numbered 1920-53, most of the units were run-in during the first half of 1932 on the Guildford via Cobham line, where they carried suburban letter headcodes. But for the opening of the first section of the Brighton line electrification, to Three Bridges and from Redhill to Reigate, numerical headcodes were introduced, setting a precedent for all subsequent main line electrification schemes. All 33 units were renumbered 2921-53 at the end of 1936, and apart from the blanking over of the louvre ventilator above the headcode panel and the fitting of electric 'raspberry' horns on the roof in place of the air-operated whistle, remained virtually unaltered until the last were withdrawn early in 1969. Unlike most other units, they kept very much to the lines for which they were built throughout their entire lives, working seemingly endless trips between Victoria or London Bridge and Brighton; unit 2923 heads another away from Victoria *(preceding page)* on the 9.47 stopping train to Brighton via Redhill on 5 June 1966. Trips away from the Brighton line were rare, and then it was only usually during times of service disruption; one such occasion was 9 December 1967, after the south had been hit by a particularly heavy fall of snow, when the camera caught an unidentified 4LAV *(below right)* heading west past Goring on a Brighton-Portsmouth working. Two additional 4LAVs, Nos 2954/5, were completed during the first half of 1940, but although the accommodation provided was the same as the earlier units, the construction and appearance followed that of the contemporary 2HAL units (see page 31) and indeed, the motor coaches were identical. They, too, spent all their working lives plying the Brighton line; unit 2955 runs into Balcombe *(above)* on the 14.12 London Bridge-Brighton on 31 May 1968. Serious war damage was confined to one unit, 2947, which was subsequently repaired, but one motor coach of unit 2926 was destroyed in the South Croydon accident of 24 October 1947, and was replaced by the motor coach from 2HAL unit No 2646, which was disbanded. However, 2926 suffered a further collision in the early 1960s, when its compartment trailer was badly damaged and replaced by an ex-4SUB augmentation all-steel vehicle, so that by 7 September 1965, when it was to be seen *(above right)* heading the 10.47 Victoria-Brighton train away from Haywards Heath, its appearance was decidedly hybrid! /*Brian Stephenson; J. Scrace (2); J. A. Vaughan*

In addition to the 2NOLs for stopping services, 10 entirely new two-car units were provided for semi-fast services to Eastbourne and Hastings in early 1935. These 2BIL units, numbered 1891-1900, were clearly developed from the 4LAV units, but both the motor coach, which also included the guards van, and the driving trailer composite had a side corridor to all compartments; each coach included a lavatory, but there was no gangway between the coaches. The front ends were very similar to those of the 4LAVs, but the cab and brake van sides were not flattened. Able to work with both the 3SUB and 2NOL units, the 2BILs soon proved their versatility, and 38 more, Nos 1901-20/54-71 appeared in late 1936 for the Portsmouth Direct and Alton line scheme. When, at the end of that year, the LAVs were renumbered into the 29XX series the BILs were also renumbered; Nos 1891-1900 became 2001-10, whilst 1901-20/54-71 became 2011-48. The second batch were very similar to the first 10 units, but had a larger brake van and only 6½ instead of 7 compartments in the motor coach. A new method of fixing the windows from the outside, first tried on the 6PAN motor coaches (see page 36) was adopted, and the louvres over the doors and cab headcode panel were dispensed with. Another batch of units, Nos 2049-2116, was built during the second half of 1937 for the Mid-Sussex scheme and was identical in almost all respects to the earlier batch except that both vehicles of 2116 were experimentally fitted with steel-panelled roofs instead of the usual wood-and-canvas variety. Finally, Nos 2117-52 were constructed in the autumn of 1938 for the Reading line electrification; again they were identical to their predecessors, save that large self-contained buffers similar to those used on the express units were fitted in place of the rather spindly variety used on all previous stock, semi-fast and suburban.

One of the first ten units, No 2002, brings up the rear of a westbound train as it restarts from Durrington-on-Sea on 11 June, 1962 *(above)*, while one of the second batch of units, with its original No 1911, and minus headcode, leads the first electrically-worked train into Woking on Sunday morning 1 November 1936 *(above right)*, some months before public services began. Posing at one of the Ascot 'race day' platforms in December 1938 *(below right)*, alongside M7 Class 0-4-4T No 379 on one of the push-pull trains it was to displace, is No 2147, one of the last batch with self-contained buffers. */A. A. Vickers; SR (2)*

1911
DANGER
DON'T TOUCH
CONDUCTOR RAILS

212
SOUTHERN
379
212
2147
38

The BILs seemed to suffer more than their fair share of war and accident damage; units 2014, 2102/31 were lost as a result of enemy action, whilst the driving trailers of 2056/69/88, 2100 and 2133 were all written off as a result of accident damage. Units 2056 and 2088 were given 1939-type 2HAL driving trailers from units 2646 and 2653 respectively (see page 31), while 2069, 2100/33 acquired entirely new driving trailers (although some were rebuilt on reclaimed underframes) similar in construction to the post-war all-steel 2HALs, but with a lower roof line to match those of the 2BILs. Unit No 2088, with 1939-type HAL driving trailer, arrives at Portsmouth & Southsea on a stopping train from Waterloo on 15 March 1960 *(above right)*, while on the same day No 2100, with all-steel driving trailer, waits at the buffers for its next working *(above)*.

The BILs worked over almost every inch of the Western and Central lines, but never on the Eastern Section; unit 2101 was clearly trying to break new ground *(below)* when it ended up on the down local at Balham after

running away from Streatham Hill sidings on 12 July 1960 and completely surmounting the buffers! But perhaps the most ignominious fate of all befell unit No 2006 in 1963; because of the urgent need for more electrically-heated suburban stock on the non-electrified Oxted line, 2006 was withdrawn from traffic, stripped of its electrical control gear and motor bogie, provided with five ex-4SUB augmentation trailers (one of which had its first class reinstated) and put to work on Oxted line peak services as locomotive-hauled seven-car set 900; it is seen *(below)* leaving Oxted on 13 September 1963 on the 17.20 London Bridge-Tunbridge Wells West. In 1966, to conform with SR trailer unit convention, it was classified 7TC and renumbered 701, although unlike all other trailer units, it was not equipped with driving controls. After the winter of 1968/69, 701 was withdrawn. The BIL vehicles were broken up but the SUB trailers have all seen further use, either in 4SUB or 4EPB units. */C. P. Boocock, S. C. Nash (2)*

BIL meets HAL *(left)*; a comparison between the rounded Maunsell 2BIL front end and the later angular, welded Bulleid front end which first appeared on the 2HAL units, of which more overleaf. Note the slender-shanked buffers on the 2BIL compared with the later, self-contained type on the 2HAL and the differing cab window styles, as well as the later BR two-tone 'raspberry' horns which both had acquired when photographed at Brighton in 1971.

For over 30 years, the green-painted BILs and, later, HALs almost became part of the scenery of Surrey, Sussex, and Hampshire, although the yellow front ends and, later, blue livery of the late 60s struck a more discordant note. Still sporting green livery—although one has already acquired a yellow face—two 2BILs and a 2HAL rattle through the open countryside *(below)* near Christ's Hospital on a Bognor-Victoria working in 1967.

Leading another of the same class away from Woking Junction towards Guildford with the 12.27 Waterloo-Portsmouth & Southsea stopping train *(right)* on 13 September 1964 is 2BIL No 2101 in a view typical of the BR 'middle period' on the Southern; the air-operated whistle has given way to electric horns, the first-class accommodation is now denoted by the continental-style yellow line at cantrail level, and the 'ferret-and-dartboard' has given way to the later coaching stock emblem although the livery is still the smart and serviceable 'multiple-unit green'.

Most of the 2BIL units were withdrawn during 1969-70, being replaced by new 4VEP units; strenuous efforts to have one preserved proved unsuccessful, and these once-ubiquitous units are now quite extinct. */Alan Williams; M. H. C. Baker; Brian Stephenson*

2101
57

For the Gillingham and Maidstone electrification of July 1939, an entirely new type of unit, the 2HAL, was produced. Numbered 2601-76, they were of the same basic construction and dimension as the BILs, but in external appearance were vastly different; the rounded front end of the BILs gave way to a stark, angular cab made up from welded steel sheet, with the motorman's cab door slightly recessed from the remainder of the curved bodyside, which featured flush-fitting windows with large-radius corners. Perhaps reflecting the outer suburban rather than semi-fast nature of the Eastern Section services, but certainly an inconvenience later, the motor coaches were designed as compartment vehicles, with only the driving trailer composites following the BIL side-corridor layout. Interior finish was more spartan, with rexine or painted panels replacing the varnished stained teak of the BILs, while the seating, especially in the compartment motor coaches, was positively uncomfortable.

Most of the units were run-in on Western and Central Section services, and towards the end of 1939, 16 further units Nos 2677-92 were constructed to enable Reading line trains, on which there had been a considerable increase in traffic, to be lengthened from six to eight cars. In contrast to the BILs, no HALs suffered serious war damage. In 1948, unit 2646 was split up, its motor coach going to 4LAV unit 2926 to replace one destroyed in the South Croydon accident (see page 22) and its driving trailer to 2BIL 2056. The driving trailer of 2653 went to unit 2088 in 1950, and was replaced early in 1951 by an all-steel driving trailer similar to those provided for BILs 2069, 2100/33.

Hurrying through the orchards near Malling *(above)* is 2HAL unit No 2663 leading two others of the same type on a Victoria-Maidstone East working on 13 May, 1947. The Eastern Section HALs were displaced in 1958 by new BR Standard 2HAP units, and were transferred to the Western and Central Sections to join the BILs and replace the NOLs, then being withdrawn.

Unit No 2608 approaches Ardingly *(above left)* on 9 May 1959 on the 14.16 Horsted Keynes-Seaford. This previously double-track branch from Haywards Heath had just been singled between Horsted Keynes and Ardingly so that the old down line could be used to stable new 4CEP and 4BEP stock for the forthcoming Kent Coast electrification; just over four years later, on 28 October 1963, the line was closed, the only Southern Electric line to suffer under the Beeching Plan.

Although the HALs, unlike the BILs, ran regularly on all three sections of the Southern, perhaps their most consistent haunt was the Reading line, where they worked for over 30 years; unit 2618 leads a 2BIL down the bank from Virginia Water to Egham *(left)* in April 1968 on a Reading-Waterloo via Richmond working.

Although most of the HALs were withdrawn in 1969/70, at the same time as the BILs, several were used as parcels units for a short time, and six, Nos 2604/5/38/45/89/92, were reclassified 2PAN and renumbered 061-6 in time for the Christmas 1970 mail traffic. Apart from occasional use as shunting units, they were put into store for the best part of 1971, reappearing for the Christmas traffic of that year before being finally withdrawn in early 1972.

/D. Birch; S. C Nash; BR

To make good the post-war shortage of two-car units caused by war and accident damage, seven additional 2HAL units, Nos 2693-99, were turned out towards the end of 1948. Accommodation was the same as the pre-War units, but the bodies were of all-steel construction, similar in appearance to the post-War 4SUBs. They had unusually large brake vans of 2 tons capacity, and this made them ideal for the Victoria-Gatwick Airport traffic when this service was inaugurated in June 1958; for the next ten years or so they could be seen plying regularly between these points attached to the London end of the half-hourly Victoria-Littlehampton/Bognor trains. But occasionally, particularly towards the end of their lives, they 'escaped' onto other workings, as did unit 2694, accelerating *(above)* downgrade from Buriton summit at the head of the six-car 12.23 Waterloo-Portsmouth stopping train on 27 January 1969.

The last 2HAL, unit 2700, did not appear until early 1955 and was formed from an eight-bay all-steel saloon motor coach from 4SUB No 4590 and a new driving trailer built at the same time as the replacements for BILs 2069, 2100/33. It was therefore the only HAL ever to have a non-compartment motor coach, although, because it did not have lavatories in both vehicles, it did not qualify as a BIL! Because of its 4SUB parentage, the motor coach of 2700 originally had only one guard's periscope, and it was therefore confined to the Eastern Section Gillingham and Maidstone Lines, where solo working of two-car units was almost unknown, until fitted with a second periscope in 1957. It was transferred to the Central and Western Section pool along with the other HALs in 1958, and on 18 July 1959 was at the head of an up Alton-Waterloo train as it pauses at Surbiton alongside 4SUB unit 4366 on a Hampton Court-Waterloo service *(below)*. Unit 2700 was disbanded in 1968, when the motor coach returned to suburban service as an accident replacement, first in 4SUB 4282 and then in 4369. */J. H. Bird; J. N. Faulkner*

Several HAL vehicles continued in traffic long after the class itself had been totally withdrawn; motor coaches from both pre-War and post-War types were used to replace accident-damaged vehicles in 4SUB units, as well as to form the power cars of additional units Nos 4131/2, although all have now been withdrawn. But the simple construction of the HAL-type motor coaches proved to be a boon when it came to conversion for use in Departmental service, and ten still survive, coupled back-to-back as de-icing units 001-3 and stores units 022/3. Introduced in 1967/8, the three de-icing units were formed from the motor coach from 2HAL 2608, the ex-HAL motor coach from 4LAV unit 2926, and the motor coaches of the 1940 HAL-style 4LAV units 2954/5. The controls have been modified so that the units may work with EP-type stock, as well as certain locomotives, and in addition to the de-icing equipment and control gear, roller blind route indicators and improved windscreen wipers have been fitted. Like their earlier ex-1925 3SUB cousins, Nos 001-3 are only normally active in the winter, being stored during the frost-free summer months. But of late, unit 001 has also been seeing service in Autumn as a water-cannon unit, equipped to spray slippery leaf-mulch off the rails. Unit 001 waits *(below)* in Guildford Yard with electro-diesel No 73 130 already attached, ready for another spraying sortie; an electro-diesel pilot is necessary because the demand for prolonged slow-speed running during such operations would cause over-heating of the emu's resistances.

In early 1970, two two-car stores units, Nos 022/3, were formed from the motor coaches of withdrawn 2HAL units Nos 2613/24/42/69; the interiors were gutted and fitted with racks for carrying spares, but although roller-blind route indicators were fitted, the controls were not modified as on the de-icing units. Both units, together with 024, formed from all-steel 4SUB power cars (see page 63), work their own weekly circular rosters which take them to all the main Southern depots; unit 023 *(above)* was photographed during its call at Wimbledon Park on 14 July 1972. */R. E. Ruffell; J. Scrace*

Front ends, 1930s style, courtesy of Messrs. Maunsell and Bulleid. The first units for main-line use, the 4LAVs introduced in 1932, had a front end based very much on contemporary suburban designs, as on 2933 *(below right)* and this was further developed for the 2BIL units of 1935-38 achieving what was probably the most pleasing of all SR front end designs, as witness unit 2016 at speed *(right)*. The Brighton line express stock had a clean, rakish front end *(below)*, but the decision to gangway the Portsmouth line stock throughout called for an upright front end, and the new 4COR units, including 3119 *(below, far right)* had virtually a normal coach end with a cab window let in one side and a headcode panel on the other; whether it was because of their 'one-eyed' look, or merely because of their association with Portsmouth is not clear, but the units quickly became known as 'Nelsons' amongst the operating staff.
With tradition thus firmly broken, the way was paved for Bulleid to produce an entirely new design of front end for his first contribution, the 2HAL units. Although the domed cab roof of earlier non-corridor units was retained, the style was entirely new; gone were the rounded corners and square-framed windows. The entire front end, including the angular roof, was of welded construction, with flush-fitting windows, and only the electrical plumbing and headcode panel relieved its stark apprarance—the electric horns in this view of unit 2661 at Reading *(below left)* were a later BR addition. But there was a slight throwback to earlier practice—the cabside doors were straight and slightly recessed from the curved bodyside of the remainder of the coach, rather like the earlier LAVs, as seen *(left)* in this comparison of 12226 of 2HAL 2641 and 11215 of 4COR 3149 at Brighton in 1971. /*Alan Williams (2); J Scrace; J H. Bird; BR.*

2933

3119
3119

In readiness for its first main-line electrification, to Brighton and Worthing at the beginning of 1933, the Southern ordered two prototype express motor coaches, Nos 11001/2, one each from Birmingham RCW Co and Metropolitan-Cammell. They were of all-steel construction, with all axles motored and at 57tons were practically electric locomotives; the front end, developed from contemporary suburban stock, was remarkably clean in line, the main difference being the complete absence of guttering above the cab windows. In addition to the motorman's cab and brake van, there were seven eight-seat bays, arranged in two saloons, with a centre gangway, giving 56 seats. Coach 11001 had straight bodysides, which were carried down to cover the solebars, as on the later Pullman stock, but 11002 had the more conventional Maunsell curved bodyside, with exposed frames. For some months in 1932 the two, with three temporarily-converted steam coaches between, ran trials as a five-car unit on the Guildford via Cobham line, although unlike the 4LAVs, they were not used in public service.
The trials were evidently a success, because 44 more motor coaches, almost identical to 11002 save for a reduction in seating of half a bay (giving 52 seats) to enable a larger van, were ordered in equal numbers from BRCW and MCW. Trailer vehicles, to orthodox Maunsell standards and on standard underframes, were built at Eastleigh, while 23 composite all-steel Pullman cars were ordered from MCW. The result was 20 six-car Pullman units classified 6PUL and originally numbered 2001-20, for everyday main-line use and three 6CIT units, Nos 2041-3, with all first-class accommodation in the trailers, for use on the 'City Limited' Brighton-London Bridge commuter service. Unit 2019 *(above)* is on a trial run prior to the introduction of electric working; note the unit number repeated low down on each corner of the front end.
The next express units, built for the Eastbourne and Hastings scheme in 1935, were very similar to the PULs, but their motor coaches had 'Airstream' sliding glass ventilators above the windows instead of the louvres and droplights of the PULs, and the composite Pullman car was replaced by a 'Pantry' or buffet first. Classified 6PAN and numbered 2021-37, the new units worked from the outset with the 6PUL units on both the existing Brighton and newly-electrified Hastings lines, thus inaugurating the standard 6PUL-6PAN formation which remained the rule on these routes for the next 30 years. Newly finished 2036, complete with white roof *(above right)*, ventures along the newly-electrified line to Eastbourne and Hastings on a trial run in early summer 1935, before the official opening on 7 July. At the end of 1936, 2001-37/41-3 were renumbered 3001-37/41-3. The two 1932 prototype motor coaches were used in 6CIT units 2041 and 2042; after the war, the demand for first-class accommodation on commuter services was less and the 'City Limited' was not resumed, so some of the first-class accommodation in what had now become units 3041-3 was downrated to third, and the units became three more 6PULs. Slab-sided prototype car No 11001 of unit 3041 *(right)* waits at Brighton for its next working north in the early 1960s. */BR (2); G. M. Kichenside*

3009
58

World War 2 inevitably affected main line services to the South Coast; in May 1942 all Pullman, restaurant and buffet services on Southern lines were withdrawn, and the Pullman cars were taken out of units 3001-20/41-3, which then ran as 5CORs until Pullman services were restored in 1946; the pantry vehicles in the 6PAN units remained in traffic, but with the catering equipment locked out of use. Only unit 3030, which was hit by a flying bomb at Brighton in 1944, suffered severe bomb damage; one trailer was completely destroyed and an entirely new replacement vehicle was built in 1946. Otherwise changes were few, and apart from the fitting of unit 3016 with electro-pneumatic brakes in 1947, mainly involved temporary switching of Pullman cars between units. Consistent complaints of rough riding culminated in a not entirely-successful programme of bogie modifications in 1956, but generally the units weathered well, as evidenced by newly-varnished 6PUL 3009 at Hastings *(preceding page)* in 1962, all but 30 years old yet little changed. When the Brighton line replacement stock, in the form of 4CIGs and 4BIGs, began to appear from York between 1964 and 1966, the PULs and PANs were gradually withdrawn. But not all were immediately sent for scrap; some were reformed into ten 6COR units, Nos 3041-50, for use on Eastern Section commuter services when the recast, more intensive timetable came into operation in July 1967. No non-EPB stock, suburban or main line, had regularly worked east of Gillingham before, so crew training runs for the South Eastern men to learn the controls of the older stock were necessary; on 11 March 1967 unit 3049, complete with electric horns, emerges from Penge Tunnel *(above)* on the 10.23 Stewarts Lane-Ramsgate training working. The comparative age of the units made them less than popular with both staff and passengers, who were used to the dubious but at least more modern delights of 4CEP units, and the 6CORs

lasted only until replacement stock was available, being withdrawn again in 1968.

The 6PULs and 6PANs were not the only express units built for the Brighton line electrification schemes; perhaps the best-known Southern Electric units of all were the three handsome five-car all-Pullman units, built in 1932 for the Victoria-Brighton 'Southern Belle' service in readiness for electrification throughout in 1933. Constructed by Metropolitan-Cammell, the three units remained the property of the Pullman Car Company until it was taken over by British Rail in 1963, but although the all-steel bodies were of traditional Pullman design, with flat sides and recessed, inward-opening doors, the electrical equipment was virtually identical to that of the 6PULs, with which they could and did work in multiple.

Classified 5BEL, the units were originally numbered 2051-3, but became 3051-3 at the same time as the other express stock was renumbered in December 1936; meanwhile, the name of the train itself was changed to the 'Brighton Belle' in 1934. All three units were taken out of traffic and stored for most of the War period, although not before one motor coach of unit 3052 had been severely damaged at Victoria in October 1940; 3051/3 were returned to traffic in 1946, and 3052, with rebuilt motor coach, in 1947.

Two of the units were normally used at a time, leaving the third available for maintenance or as a standby; occasionally, the third unit would be used for a Royal Special or, at busy periods, pressed into ordinary service along with one of the other express units. It is after one such sortie with a 6PUL unit that 3052 is taking the Quarry line at Coulsdon North *(above)* on an empty stock working to Lovers Walk, Brighton in March 1960.

Although they spent their entire lives making the thrice-daily 50 mile non-stop dash from Victoria to Brighton and back, because of their six-year sojourn

PULLMAN
3052
4
54

during the war, the BELs were not considered life-expired when the remainder of the original express stock was withdrawn in 1965/6 and in 1968/9 they were refurbished and modernised internally, while the traditional Pullman chocolate and cream livery, carried by unit 3052 *(above left)* as it heads away from Clapham Junction on a down working on 9 June, 1968, gave way to the more modernistic but certainly less attractive rail blue and grey the same unit sports—together with a roller-blind route indicator—as it rolls into Brighton *(above)* with the 14.00 from Victoria on 21 March, 1972, just a month before the Pullman services were withdrawn and replaced with rather less romantic 4CIGs and 4BIGs.

But they did not pass unnoticed; their last runs in public service, on Sunday, 30 April 1972, brought out crowds all along the route to pay their last respects, while the enthusiast societies had a field day organising rail tours to corners of the electrified system never before (or since!) blessed with such imposing stock; unit 3053 brakes for the speed restriction at Ford *(left)* on 8 April 1972 whilst on the Bognor-Littlehampton leg of a marathon tour from Waterloo which also took in Portsmouth, Brighton, Eastbourne and Ore. And in stark contrast to almost every other type of Southern unit, hardly a single vehicle has been cut up; although the units have been split up into single vehicles, all have been preserved in one form or another—some on preserved lines and others as speciality restaurants at places far removed from their familiar tramping ground. */Alan Williams; B. Stephenson; G. M. Kichenside; J. H. Cooper-Smith (2); J. Scrace*

Of all the types of Southern Electric stock, main line or suburban, none experienced so many changes, or worked on such a variety of services as the 'Nelsons' or 'Pompeys' —the four-car corridor units originally built for the Portsmouth Direct and Mid-Sussex schemes of 1937 and 1938. Experience with the Brighton line express units had shown that, while they were mechanically and electrically sound, their six-car formation and lack of gangways between units was an operating inconvenience, while the sheer weight of the motor coaches—59tons on the production version—punished the track. So, ever mindful of economy (and the Portsmouth Direct scheme was conceived during the depression) the Southern Board opted for four-car, scaled-down, lightweight—and, some will say, underpowered—versions of the Brighton units. The trailer cars were similar to the earlier stock, but the motor coaches, although identical in seating plan, were built at Eastleigh rather than by a contractor, and reverted to the traditional wood framed, steel panelled method of body construction, with wood and canvas roofs, and only one 450hp motor bogie instead of two. But the greatest innovation was the complete break with previous practice in favour of a gangwayed front end, to allow continuous passage throughout a train formed of several units. Gone was the traditional domed front end in favour of an upright design with one rather small cab window and a somewhat cramped motorman's cab on one side, and the headcode stencil panel on the other. Why the Southern chose to forsake the standard Pullman gangway and associated buck-eye coupling used on all its contemporary steam stock in favour of its own capacious but rather complicated design of gangway, together with screw couplings, for its electric stock has never been adequately explained; certainly in later years, when the units had been downgraded to semi-fast duties, it led to endless problems during coupling and uncoupling.

For the Portsmouth direct electrification of 1937, 29 four-car corridor units (4COR) Nos 3101-29 were

provided, together with 18 four-car restaurant units (4RES), Nos 3054-72; these latter had the same motor coaches as the CORs, but had compartment/dining saloon first and kitchen/dining saloon second trailers in place of the composite and second trailers of the former. Heading an eight-car Waterloo-Portsmouth Harbour express round the curves near Haslemere *(below left)* on 17 March 1938, nine months after full services began, is 4COR unit 3116, carrying, as did all the Portsmouth Expresses for many years, the highly misleading "Waterloo-Portsmouth-Isle of Wight" roofboards. Staff at Portsmouth Harbour spent many weary hours disillusioning passengers happily remaining in the train after arrival in the fond belief that it was about to board a train ferry and take them without change to their Island holiday destinations! For the Mid-Sussex scheme of 1938, 26 more 4COR units, Nos 3130-55, were built, together with 13 new buffet units (4BUF) Nos 3073-85. Instead of the restaurant/kitchen cars of the 4RES units, the 4BUFs had a pressure-ventilated full-length buffet of strikingly modernistic design—one of the first manifestations of the Bulleid regime!

The decision to provide full restaurant facilities to Portsmouth was probably a mistake; traffic declined over the years, and three restaurant cars written off during the war were not replaced. Rumours were rife for many years that the cars would be converted to buffets, but apart from the rebuilding of the kitchen of 3072 as a buffet in 1956 after fire damage two years previously, it was not until 1962 that the restaurant cars of units 3056/65/8 were rebuilt as handsome Griddle cars; as can be seen from 12605 of 3056 *(below)* the job was done thoroughly, with completely new bodysides incorporating BR-Standard shape windows. As a result, the units were reclassified 4GRI, and when the remainder of the RES units were withdrawn two years later 3056/65/8 remained in traffic and were renumbered 3086-8. */SR; Alan Williams*

The Portsmouth units suffered more than most from the rigours of war; in all, 25 vehicles were destroyed or damaged beyond repair. One of the most spectacular incidents was the bombing of Portsmouth Harbour Station in January 1941, severely damaging several units; as a result of this 'blitz, the pier was isolated from the mainland, and for security reasons it was allowed to remain so until after the War. The undamaged stock remained marooned there for five years until lifted out by crane in 1946. All the damaged stock was repaired, and the 25 vehicles written off were replaced by new vehicles built to the same designs at Eastleigh in 1946 and virtually indistinguishable from their pre-war sisters. The restaurant cars of damaged units 3058/60/3 were not replaced, and their motor coaches were used to form three additional 4CORs, Nos 3156-8.

In January 1964 there was a major reorganisation of stock; the 4RES units were withdrawn and replaced on the Portsmouth Direct line by 4BUF units transferred from the Mid-Sussex line, but while the kitchen seconds were sent for scrap, the motor coaches and trailer diner firsts were reformed with Pullman or trailer second cars from withdrawn PUL and PAN units to form 4PUL units 3054-7/9 and 4COR(N) units 3066-71 for use on the Central Section during the switch to 4CIG and 4BIG working. Restarting from Haywards Heath (*above right*) are 4COR(N) 3066 and a 4PUL on the 11.25 Victoria-Littlehampton on 7 September 1965. These units were themselves all withdrawn by March 1966; the Pullmans and trailer diner firsts went for scrap, but the motor coaches were reformed yet again, this time with further trailer seconds and trailer composites from withdrawn PULs and PANs to form 10 additional 4COR units Nos 3159-68. Readily distinguished from the original 4CORs by the louvred doors of its trailers, 3159 sets out down the slow line from Woking *(above)* on a peak hour Waterloo-Alton working in early 1968.

The art of keeping the deadman's handle depressed while depositing the single-line token is amply demonstrated *(right)* by the motorman of 4COR 3153 on the 14.04 Guildford-Waterloo via Ascot as it comes off the single track section from Ash Vale at Frimley Junction on 23 October 1971, by which time the 4CORs had displaced the 2BILs and 2HALs on Reading line services. /*Alan Williams; J. Scrace; G. P. Cooper*

One of the most interesting of the many reformations that occurred during the life of the 4CORs also brought Brighton line stock to the Western Section; in June 1965, as a result of accident damage, one motor coach each in units 3124/48 was replaced by a motor coach from withdrawn 6PUL units 3017/8. This was the first occasion since the trials of 1932 that Brighton-line motor coaches had performed on the Western Section, and this super-powered pair put up some fine runs, both on their weekday rush hour Waterloo-Farnham workings—during one of which 3124 leads 3148 *(above)* past Clapham Junction on the 19.17 Waterloo-Farnham on 15 July, 1964—and on summer Saturdays when formed with a 4BUF between for use on Waterloo-Portsmouth relief trains.

The business end of a 4COR motor coach *(left)*; this 1971 view of 11215 of 3149 shows the suspension of the gangway, with its typical slightly-forward leaning stance, and the equalising beam motor bogie with the later type of shoegear.

The winters of 1962 and 1963 were particularly severe, and caused widespread dislocation to the Southern's electric services. With its shoegear arcing furiously *(right)*, an anonymous snow-covered 4COR swings across to the slow line at Surbiton with the much-delayed 08.50 Waterloo-Portsmouth Harbour one day in January 1962; as can be seen, the adjacent down through line had been abandoned to the elements. */B. Stephenson; Alan Williams (2)*

ACTON CENTRAL
3135
75
3135
WARNING
KEEP OFF
ELECTRIC
LIVE RAILS

3159
3159
ESTATE AGENTS
SYMONDS
WOTE STREET
BASINGSTOKE

By the time the 4CORs were finally withdrawn from traffic at the end of September 1972, representatives of the class had traversed just about every major Southern electrified route as well as—thanks to the initiative of some enthusiasts' groups—one or two others! Following the conversion of the ex-LNWR Broad Street-Richmond and Euston-Watford third-and-fourth rail system to purely third rail, the LCGB organised a special from Richmond which took 3135 to such unlikely places as Willesden and Watford as well as Euston itself; the special approaches Acton Central *(above left)* on 8 November 1970.

Because of the increased line voltage—850V instead of 750V—on the Bournemouth line west of Pirbright Junction, pre-1951 stock, including the 4CORs, was banned for normal operating purposes, although stock could be worked to and from Eastleigh for repairs provided the heating circuits were disconnected. Luckily, it was high summer when two 4VEPs collided with a derailed freight train at Surbiton on 11 July, 1971, completely blocking the main line for the remainder of the day and most of the next, so 4COR 3159 *(left)* could be pressed into service on the emergency shuttle workings and is seen here after arrival at Basingstoke from Woking.

And if Watford was the northernmost extremity of 4COR operation and Basingstoke as far west as they went, the eastern extremities were covered during the SEG tour of 1 October 1972 by 3102/43, which visited Sheerness as well as Dover Marine *(above)*.

Despite their evident popularity, only one 4COR unit has survived the scrap merchants' torch; No 3142 has been preserved by the Southern Electric Group, although regrettably it is now housed far from conductor rail on the Nene Valley line near Peterborough.

COR! Birds eye view along the corridor of a 4COR trailer second *(left)*, worms eye view of 2BIL 2112, 4COR 3167 and 4CEP 7109 through the railings at Eastbourne *(below)*, and drivers view of the master controller, brake gauge and speedometer of a 4COR when first introduced in 1937 *(right)*. Braking for the 40mph speed restriction through Clapham Junction *(next page)* is 4COR 3115 on the 13.50 Waterloo-Portsmouth Harbour on 10 April, 1970. /*Michael Baker (2); SR; J. H. Cooper-Smith*

3115
3115
82

With the outbreak of War in 1939, the Southern's rolling programme of electrification, which had been virtually continuous for over 15 years, came to an abrupt halt, and the teams so painstakingly built up by Herbert Walker dispersed to other essential duties.
As it transpired, no further electrification work was undertaken for an unforgivable 20 years, and the next two decades were to be dominated by the replacement of the ageing fleet of suburban stock. Curiously, the first replacement stock, for the 1½mile Waterloo and City Line tube from Waterloo to the Bank, was already under construction at the outbreak of War. The original stock *(top right)* built in the USA and assembled at Eastleigh was life expired, so the Southern ordered 12 new motor coaches and 16 trailers from English Electric.
Outwardly, the new vehicles bore a striking resemblance to London Transport's 1938 Tube Stock, although the doors and ends were of unpainted aluminium. The motor coaches, like their predecessors, were double-ended so that they could be used singly in slack hours, and the frames were raised over the motor bogie, as on Car 54 *(right)* on test at Wimbledon prior to entering service in October 1940; the new cars could not be adequately tested underground before entering service because the Southern took the opportunity to resignal the line and to move the third rail from its original position between the running lines to the standard position over the single weekend of 25-27 October 1940. In peak hours, the 'Drain', as it is sometimes less than affectionately known by commuters, is operated by five-car trains formed of three trailers flanked by a motor coach at each end. No unit numbers are carried.
There has been some speculation that, when replaced, the Waterloo & City cars will be transferred to that everlasting rolling museum, the Isle of Wight, to replace the oldest stock in regular passenger use on BR, the ex-London Transport Tube stock which was transferred there when the remaining line from Ryde to Shanklin was electrified 'on the cheap' in 1967. Orthodox Southern electric stock could not be used because of clearance and length limitations. Apart from conversion to third-rail operation, refurbishing and repainting in rail blue, the tube stock, some of which dates from 1924, remains in original condition. Formed into five three-car (3TIS) and six four-car (4VEC) units Nos 031-5 and 041-6, the units normally run together (as a VEC-TIS!) to form seven-car trains in the summer. One such formation, with 4VEC 041 leading 3TIS No 031, crosses from the sidings to the up line at Ryde St Johns Road *(above left)* on 30 July, 1975 and makes for Ryde Pier Head. The ex-SECR signalbox in the background is itself second-hand, having been brought over from the mainland piecemeal in 1928 after being rendered redundant at Waterloo by the 1926 Eastern Section electrification and resignalling. */M. Hall; BR (2)*

E

Ever since the introduction of the South Western electric services in 1915, it had been the almost universal practice on all Southern suburban electric lines to provide peak hour services by strengthening the basic 3SUB formation by the addition of a two-coach trailer unit and another 3SUB, making an eight-car train. Like most of the suburban electric stock, the trailer units were converted from pre-Grouping steam stock; they had no driving cabs but were fitted with ordinary buffers at the outer ends. Careful diagramming was necessary in order to ensure that trailer units got correctly formed between motored units, and at times of out-of-course running, things would inevitably go awry; it was not unknown for a single 3SUB to have to "run round" its trailer unit at its destination before returning. Whether it was the additional pressure of wartime operating conditions, or simply a rather belated recognition of the blindingly obvious, we shall probably never know, but early in the War it was decided to abandon the 'trailer unit' concept and remarshal the trailers within the motor units, making them 4SUBs. Thus it was that, late in 1941, the first entirely new suburban unit since the 1925 stock appeared as 4SUB No 4101; it was the epitome of Bulleid pack-'em-in design, with nine compartments of incredibly narrow dimensions in the motor coaches, 11 in the trailer third and 10—six first flanked by two lots of two third—in the trailer composite. The welded front end, cab sides and domed roof were virtually identical to those of the 1939 2HAL units, but the remainder of the bodyside was of an entirely new contour, gently but continuously curved from cantrail to solebar and to the maximum the loading gauge would allow so as to give six-a-side seating per compartment. Just before 4101 went into service on the South Eastern Division, first class was abolished on all suburban lines, so its composite was never used as such; it was joined by a second unit, No 4102, in 1944, and eight more, Nos 4103-10, were built in 1945, including 4105 *(below)* pictured when new at Eastleigh.

All 10 units survived until the entire batch was withdrawn in 1971, although one motor coach of 4103, written off in a collision at Norwood Junction in 1968, was replaced by a 2HAL motor coach from 2644. And one motor coach survived for a few months into 1972 when it was temporarily switched to unit 4355, here approaching Wandsworth Common on the 13.41 Victoria-West Croydon on 29 March *(below right)*. Although strictly unrelated to 4101-10, it is convenient to mention here that two further units of similar appearance, Nos 4131/2, were formed in 1969 by matching the motor coaches of withdrawn 2HAL units with surplus augmentation trailers from other withdrawn units; 4131 passes Selhurst *(right)* in April 1970 on an Epsom-London Bridge working. Both units were withdrawn in October of the following year.

Units 4101-10 were very quickly nicknamed 'Queen of Shebas' (she had, we are told, 'a very great train') but complaints began to come in about the narrowness of the compartments; passengers sat with their knees almost touching and it was virtually impossible to stand in, leave alone get in or out of, a crowded compartment. So, Mr.

Bulleid relented, and the next batch of ten units, Nos 4111-20, turned out in 1946, had wider compartments, with the result that there was one less compartment in both motor and trailer coaches than in 4101-10—less seats but at least somewhere to stand!

But the major difference was at the front end; gone for good was the traditional domed front end and instead the curved bodyside of the earlier stock was continued forward to meet a slightly bowed, upright front end which, as can be seen from 4111, photographed *(next page, right)* when new in May 1946, in addition to the unit number carried the word 'SOUTHERN' in sunshine lettering above the cab windows. Gone, too, were the wood and canvas roofs, perpetuated even on 4101-10. Apart from the PUL and PAN motor coaches, 4111 was the first all-steel unit and set the standard for all subsequent SR construction, as well as heavily influencing BR Standard designs. Ten more units, Nos 4121-30, quickly followed towards the end of 1946; in external appearance they were identical to 4111-20, but internally, apart from the trailer composite, the compartments gave way to open saloons—two of four bays each in the motor coaches and three, of three, four and three bays, in the trailers. The last unit of the batch, 4130, was turned out early in 1947, and was experimentally equipped with lightweight motors of only 185hp; in 1955 they were replaced by the conventional 275hp variety with which the remainder of the batch were fitted.

The next batch of units, Nos 4355-77, built in 1947/8, rather surprisingly reverted to the all-compartment layout, although one trailer of 4377 was turned out with a single ten-bay saloon; happily the ugly and rather cumbersome advertisement panels across the luggage racks were not repeated, but the basic layout became standard for most later units, including the next batch, 4378-87, which appeared in late 1948 with two eight-bay saloon motor coaches, one 10-bay saloon trailer and a ten compartment trailer. Both the 43XX batches were easily distinguished from earlier (and subsequent) units by the grab handles mounted above and beside the cab windows, as on 4362 seen leaving Waterloo *(top)* on 30 July 1949 on a Kingston roundabout service. Note the 'British Railways' version of the earlier Southern sunshine lettering, and the 'S' prefix to the unit number.

At the very end of 1948, the first of 23 more units, Nos 4277-99, appeared; this batch was identical in body layout to the 4378-87 series, but was equipped with lightweight 250hp motors (as compared to the 275hp orthodox type fitted to the earlier units). They were immediately followed in 1949 by a further 46 units, Nos

4621-66, again of identical design and layout, but built on the salvaged frames of withdrawn 3SUB units. By now, the wholesale withdrawal of the pre-war units was releasing numbers of all-steel augmentation trailers (see pages 12-19) which were only a few years old; early in 1950, 15 more saloon motor coaches were built and paired with these redundant compartment trailers to form the seven units 4601-7; the last of the batch, 4607, looks decidedly chilly *(above left)* at Hampton Court in the depths of winter 1962. The remaining motor coach was initially used to form one end of the hybrid, partly exLBSC unit 4590, and when this was withdrawn in 1954 went to 2HAL No 2700 (see page 32) before returning to suburban work in units 4282 and 4369!

The final, and largest, batch of units, Nos 4667-4754, were turned out in 1950 and early 1951. They included one salvaged augmentation compartment trailer apiece, and the remaining vehicles were of the saloon type, identical to the 4621-66 series; all but a few were mounted on salvaged ex-3SUB frames.

Unit 4718, one of several of this batch built with roller-blind headcode panels, poses alongside

earlier 4386 *(top left)* at Crystal Palace on 1 June 1974. Changes in formation amongst the SUBs have been legion, with the result that many of the batch formations described here have become altered over the years. With the introduction of newer stock and reductions in service, many units have been withdrawn. Because compartment stock is particularly prone to vandalism, most of the units selected for withdrawal have been the earlier compartment type (in general, ironically, those with the newest underframes), while the remaining units have in most cases had their compartment trailers replaced by saloon vehicles from withdrawn units.

Some of the withdrawn units have found further use; two modified 4SUB motor coaches have been used to form an additional stores unit. No 024, seen *(bottom left)* at Eastleigh in May 1973, works on circuit diagrams with the two 2HAL conversions (see page 33), while a complete unit has been modified as four car instruction unit 055, to replace the ageing ex-3SUB 053 (see page 19).

Finally, before passing into the British Railways era proper, mention should be made of the Southern's ill-fated excursion into double-deck or, more correctly, split-deck, trains. After the War, despite the gradual introduction of the new all-steel 4SUBs with six-a-side seating, there were loud and persistent complaints of overcrowding, especially on the South Eastern section services into Charing Cross and Cannon Street. Bulleid devised an ingenious split level arrangement whereby each low level compartment, in addition to providing 11 seats, gave access via a short stairway to a further 11 in an upper saloon. The two experimental units, 4DD Nos 4001/2, were built to the absolute maximum of the loading gauge and were restricted to the three routes from Charing Cross and Cannon Street to Dartford and Gravesend, except when working to and from works. Because of restricted clearances, the upper deck windows were fixed and the compartments pressure-ventilated—not always, especially in summer, to the satisfaction of the travelling public! Amidst a fanfare of publicity, the new train was inaugurated on 1 November 1949 and, after a few teething troubles, the two units settled down to reliable service. But it soon became obvious that the principle was wrong; passengers complained that they had less room and less comfortable seats, and that the ventilation was inadequate, while operating staff were dismayed at the heavy route restriction and the additional time taken at station stops to load and unload. So, after a year's trial, it was decided late in 1950 that no more 'double-deckers' would be built, and to embark instead on a scheme to lengthen trains to 10 cars, leaving 4001/2 as rather freakish twins—which, because of their electro-pneumatic brake, could not work with other units—plying back and forth between London and Dartford each day until withdrawn in 1971; on one of many such trips 4001 waits at Borough Market Junction *(above)* for a path into Cannon Street on an up afternoon working from Dartford via Bexleyheath in summer 1963. For a few months before their withdrawal in 1971, 4001/2 were renumbered 4901/2 to make way for the prototype PEP units then entering traffic. */SR (2); J. Scrace (2); Michael Baker; Alan Williams (2); R. I. Wallace; G. M. Kichenside*

Late in 1951, the first unit of an entirely new era of rolling stock appeared from Eastleigh. Classified 4EPB and numbered 5001, the accommodation and basic bodystructure was identical to the later 4SUBs, and like them also, it was based on salvaged underframes.
But there the similarity ended; the new unit had electro-pneumatic brakes and control gear, supplied from a motor generator set mounted beneath the floor. At last, the automatic buck-eye coupling, for so long used only on SR steam stock, made an appearance, and as all the brake and control jumper cables were mounted at cab height and duplicated on each side, it was possible for the first time to couple and uncouple units entirely at platform level. The cab layout, too, marked an important departure from previous practice; there were no exterior doors to the motorman's cab, access being gained via a centre door to the adjacent guards van, and roller blind headcode panels were fitted as standard.
At first 5001 was unique, not being able to work with any other type of stock, but it was soon joined in 1952 by Nos 5002-15, and they were put to work initially on the Guildford via Cobham line, then still third class only. Construction continued unabated over the next few years; 5016-48 appeared in 1953 and 5049-53 in 1954. In 1953, two units in a new series, 5101/2, were turned out; they were identical to the earlier units, but were mounted on Central-type motor bogies—to which, incidentally, all the earlier units on Eastern bogies were converted in the early 60s. By the end of 1957, 213 units, Nos 5001-53, 5101-5260, had been built, and all but five—Nos 5023, 5103/41/67, 5204, written off or disbanded because of accident damage, survive. The 4EPBs regularly work on all three sections, often in conjunction with semi-fast stock to the coast.
Seen here clockwise *(from bottom left)* are 5015 and two

BR Standard 2HAPs approaching Woking whilst returning empty to Waterloo on 13 September 1964, having worked down to Aldershot on a special for the Farnborough Air Show; 5104 traversing a pleasant, leafy stretch of line near Thames Ditton whilst on a Waterloo-Hampton Court working on 23 September, 1973; 5160 in the double-sided platform at Sevenoaks ready to return to London on the 14.29 to Holborn Viaduct on 24 January 1975; and 5239 accelerating out of the Chertsey line platforms onto the Reading line at Virginia Water in summer 1962, before the appearance of red blinds in the headcode panels and the abolition of oil tail lamps.
All the later units, including both 5160 and 5239, had their roofs extended downwards to an additional rainstrip at cantrail level so as to match the newly-introduced BR Standard 2EPB units for the Eastern Section 10-car train scheme. Two additional units, 5261/2, were formed in 1965/6 from spare motor coaches from disbanded BR Standard 2EPB units and SR trailers from accident-damaged 4EPB and 4SUB units. More recently, a start has been made on forming further additional units, from 5263 onwards, from the motor coaches of withdrawn SR 2HAP units and converted trailers from withdrawn 4SUB units.
/B. Stephenson; D. Griffiths; R. I. Wallace; Alan Williams

IRGINIA
WATER

In 1960, the first of 56 BR Standard 4EPB units to replace the 1925 Western and Eastern Section units 4301-55 was rolled out at Eastleigh. Units 5301/2, like 5261/2 described on the previous page, had BR Standard motor coaches and spare ex-SR trailers from damaged or disbanded 4EPB and 4SUB units, but Nos 5303-56 had BR Standard trailers of somewhat unusual design, being part a five-bay saloon and part five compartments. The motor coaches are virtually identical in layout and design to those of the earlier BR 2EPB units (see page 70). In 1962/3, 14 more units, 5357-70, were built, ostensibly for Western Section use, but it was not long before they, too, gravitated to the Eastern/Central Section pool, partly because their greater length caused berthing problems at some South Western country termini. One motor coach of 5352 was written off as early as October 1962 as a result of collision damage and its place was taken by the motor coach from BR Standard 2EPB 5800, which was disbanded. The different contour of Bulleid and BR Standard stock is well illustrated by 5302 *(above)*, with its SR-type trailers, pulling away from Clapham Junction on 18 September 1974 on a Victoria-West Croydon-Wimbledon-Holborn Viaduct working.
Originally, the first units had their twin air horns mounted on the front end, one above each cab window, including 5303 *(above right)*, leaving Shortlands on a Holborn Viaduct-Sevenoaks via Catford and Swanley working on wintry 29 December 1962. This innovation was clearly less than successful, and all the units so fitted now have their horns mounted in the orthodox position on the leading edge of the roof.
Working on the same route, but a little further down at Bickley in the high summer of August 1975, is 5359 *(right)* one of the last batch of units and discernible from its predecessors by the shallower headcode panel.
/B. Morrison; O. W. Herbert; K. Lane

83
5359
83

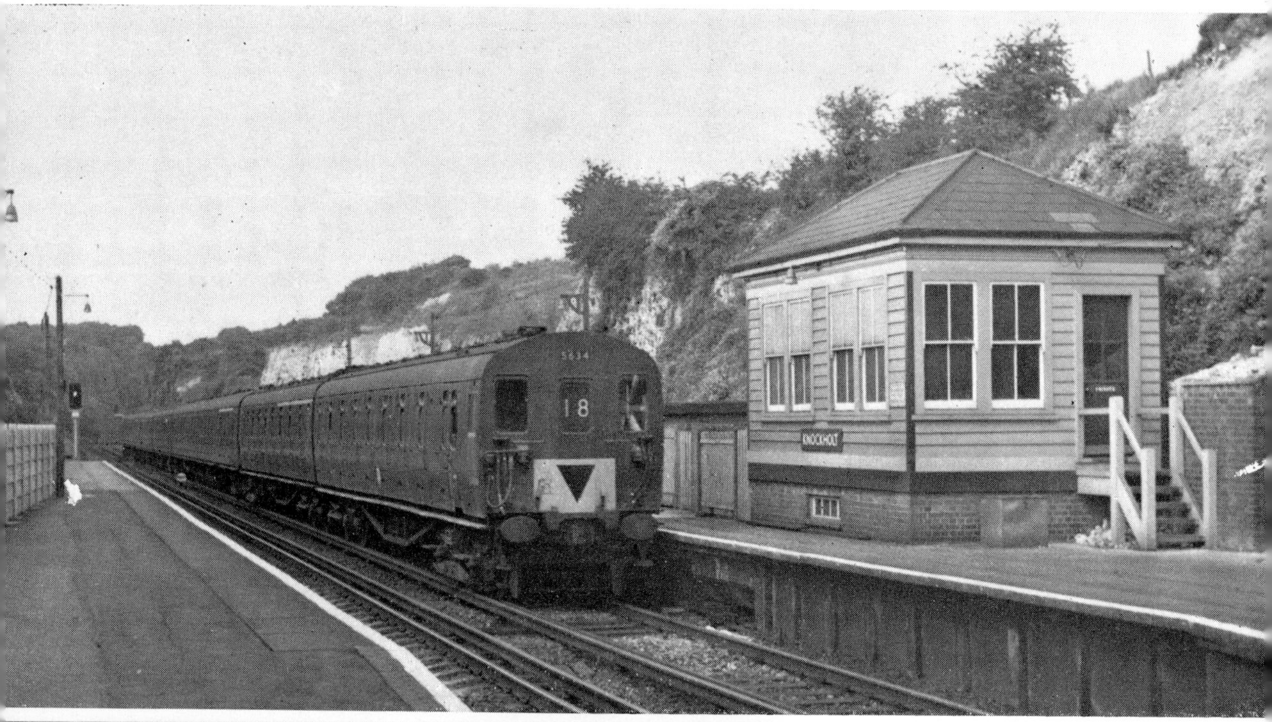

18
KNOCKHOLT

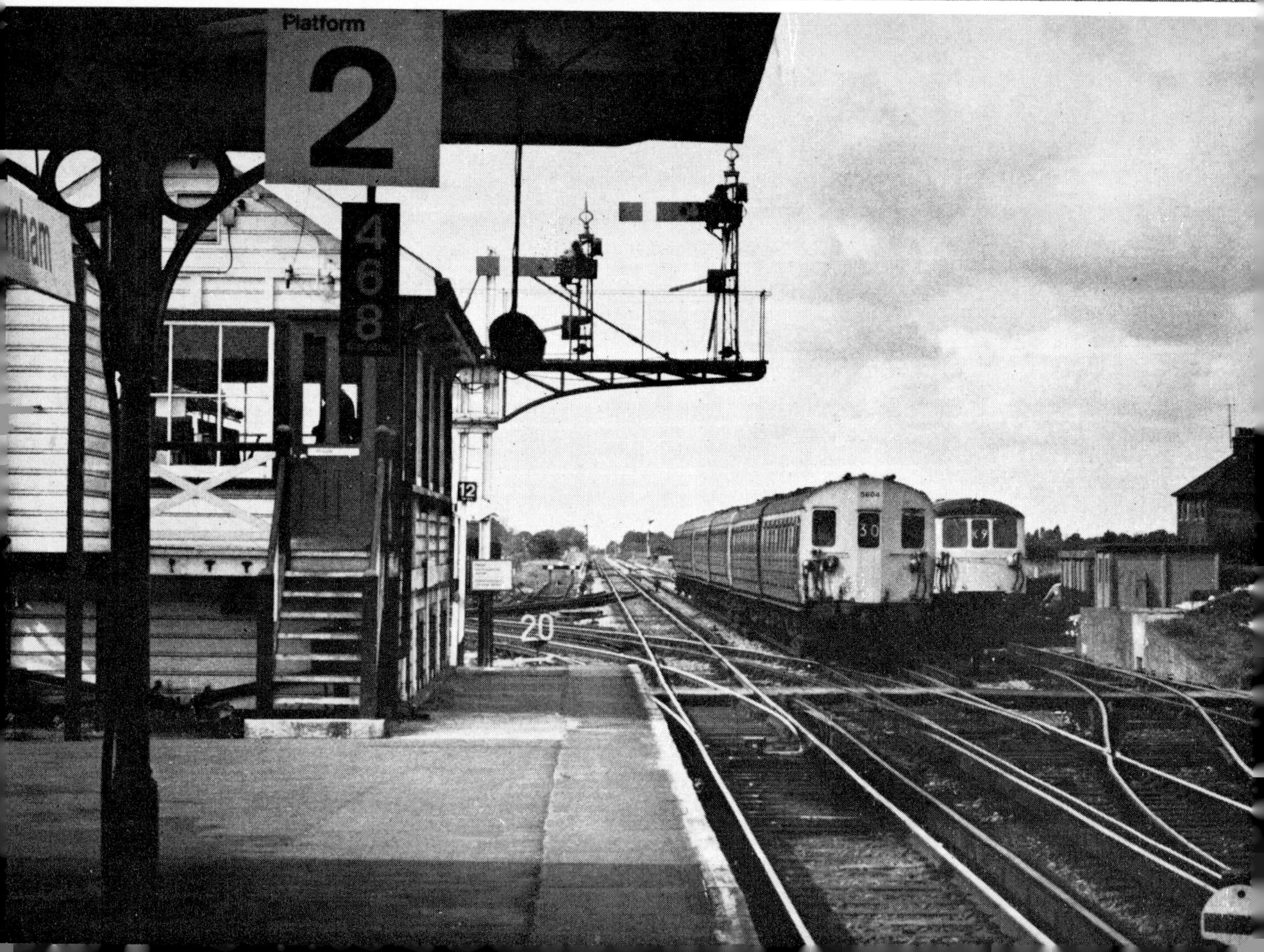

Platform
2
468
30
20

Such was the advance planning of the Southern rolling stock programme that new units to basically SR design were still being turned out at Eastleigh over a decade after Nationalisation. The last units to appear before the jigs were finally dismantled were two distinct batches of two car semi-fast (2HAP) and suburban (2EPB) units, both built on salvaged underframes from withdrawn 2NOL units. Ironically, they post-dated by several years the first BR Standard units of these designations. The 2HAP units, Nos 5601-36, were turned out in 1957/8 for use on the Eastern Section electrification extensions into Thanet; the motor coaches were virtually identical to those of the SR 4EPBs, save that the saloon was divided into two by a central partition, giving two four-bay saloons, one smoking, one non-smoking, while the driving trailer layout was similar to that used for the post-war all-steel 2HAL units (page 32), with a lavatory and side corridor giving access to 3 first class but only 4½ second class compartments, the half compartment being lost due to the need for the somewhat wasteful transverse bay immediately behind the driving cab simply to provide access to this doorless domain. All 36 units were originally equipped with express gear ratio motors, the only Bulleid design stock to be so fitted; after a decade of work on the South Eastern Division, a general reorganisation of stock working in the late 1960s brought them to the South Western Division, where in 1969 5602-5/7-9/15-8/22/34/5 suffered the ignominy of downgrading to second class only and reclassification as 2SAP for suburban use, the first-class compartments having their mats removed and armrests stitched up, whilst the lavatories were locked out of use. The original plan was to downgrade the lot, but late in 1969 there was evidently a change of plan; no more units were so treated and by the summer of 1970 all had reverted to their original condition. They were next transferred en masse to Brighton for use on the South Coast lines to replace withdrawn BILs and HALs, but in 1976 they returned to suburban work, and a start has been made on disbanding them, the driving trailers being withdrawn while the motor coaches are paired with trailers from withdrawn 4SUBs to form additional SR-type 4EPB units numbered from 5263 onwards. The SR 2HAPs were immediately followed off the assembly line at Eastleigh in 1958/9 by 34 2EPB units Nos 5651-84. Built to replace the NOLs on the Waterloo-Windsor and Weybridge lines, they were the first units to be of entirely saloon layout; the motor coaches were identical to those of the 2HAPs save for the fitting of suburban gear ratio motors, while the driving trailer was virtually an ordinary saloon trailer with a cab and transverse passageway at one end instead of a passenger bay. Although able to work with other stock, these units had a monopoly of services on the Windsor and Weybridge lines until fairly recently, when they were transferred away to other South Western Suburban duties, as well as working on the South London line and the London Bridge-Tattenham Corner/Caterham services.

Anticlockwise *(from top left)*, 2HAP 5634 hurries through Knockholt on the 12.10 Charing Cross-Margate on 11 September 1968; 2HAP 5604 rattles into Barnham on 10 September 1974 on the 11.03 Portsmouth Harbour-Brighton, passing Class 73 No 73 127 no an up van train; and 2EPB 5667 waits in the bay platform at Weybridge while mail traffic is loaded prior to return to Waterloo via Staines and Richmond in Summer 1963. */J. Scrace; R. I. Wallace; Alan Williams*

5757

The first BR Standard stock constructed for the Southern electric lines was the batch of 78 2EPB units, Nos 5701-78, built between 1954 and 1956 to allow the lengthening of Eastern Section rush hour trains to 10 cars, and to replace the ageing converted exLBSCR ac overhead stock on the South London and Wimbledon-West Croydon routes. Unit 5707 waits at Charing Cross *(below)* to depart for Dartford shortly after introduction. Note the additional 'plumbing' on the front end which, as on the SR 4EPB units, was later removed when the control cable arrangements were rationalised. In construction similar to the contemporary BR Standard non-corridor locomotive-hauled stock, and with front ends based very much on the SR 4EPB design, but with a flatter profile and overhanging roof, the units provided 186 seats in two four-bay saloons in the motor coach and one such saloon plus five separate compartments in the driving trailer.
Unit 5766 was destroyed in the Lewisham disaster in December 1957 and was replaced by an additional unit, 5779, built in 1958; a further unit, 5800, was formed in 1960.
At the same time that the SR units were being built, Eastleigh also turned out 15 basically similar units for the then North Eastern Region South Tyneside services, but with a larger brake van and therefore one less compartment in the motor coach, a solitary first-class compartment in the driving trailer, and a destination blind panel and five-lamp route indicator instead of the standard SR headcode panel. When the South Tyneside lines were de-electrified in 1963, the redundant units were transferred to the SR; the first-class compartment was downrated to second and the destination and route-lamp panels were replaced by a headcode panel before they entered service as units 5781-95. Recognisable by their smaller headcode panel as well as their larger brake van, these units have worked mainly on the Central and Western Sections because of their reduced accommodation; 5791 approaches Dundonald Road Crossing *(left)* on a mid-day Wimbledon-West Croydon working in summer 1970. Towards the end of 1964, 5701/4/8/9/11, 5800 were disbanded, their driving trailers being used in 3R diesel-electric units 1201-5, while their motor coaches were used to replace accident-damaged vehicles in 4EPB units 5247 and 5352 and, with spare SR-type trailers, to form two additional 4EPB units, Nos 5261/2.
With the recent widespread reduction of many South Western Division suburban services to six cars, even in rush hours, the 2EPB units have gained regular workings on all three Divisions; 5757 brings up the rear of an up Windsor line suburban working *(below left)* as it curves past Vauxhall on the brick viaduct approach to Waterloo on 4 Novembar 1975. */Alan Williams; F. R. Kerr*

To replace the 2HAL units on the Gillingham and Maidstone line, 42 new 2HAP units, Nos 6001-42, were built at Eastleigh in 1957/8; the motor coaches are identical to those of the 2EPB units 5701-79, except that they have express gear ratio, but the driving trailers have a five-bay second class saloon, two intermediate lavatories, and three first class compartments with a side corridor; one lavatory serves the second class accommodation, the other the first and there is no access from one class of accommodation to the other.

Like all the SR-type EPB stock and the BR Standard 2EPBs, 6001-42 were classified '1951 Stock', having electro-pneumatic contactor control. Later in 1958, the first of 63 further units, Nos 6043-6105, appeared for work on the Thanet lines then being electrified. These units had camshaft control and were termed '1957' Stock'.

For the second phase of the Kent Coast electrification, 41 more units Nos 6106-46 were built in 1961 and the final batch, 6147-73 for strengthening on the South Western and Central Divisions, appeared in 1963. Although identical in accommodation, the various batches can be recognised by their roofs; the Margate-Victoria train at Chislehurst Junction *(above)* illustrates the point, for the leading unit, 6036, is one of the first batch of '1951' stock, with exterior cabling, the next is one of the first '1957' stock units, while the centre unit, with the distinctive, slightly angled additional rainstrip is one of the final batch, Nos 6147-73.

The 2HAPs are a ubiquitous breed, and are to be found on all three sections on a wide range of work, although they are often used singly for branch line use, as was 6055 *(below)* leaving Paddock Wood for Maidstone on a

Tonbridge-Strood working shortly after the introduction of electric working in 1962. In addition to the distinctive rain strip on the roof, the last batch of units have Commonwealth bogies and a shallower headcode panel than their predecessors, seen on 6166 *(above)* as it comes over the crossing and into Southease and Rodmell Halt at the head of the 15.30 Brighton-Seaford on 6 September 1972.

Because of the influx of new 4VEP units and the demise of older suburban stock, the Southern found itself in 1973/4 with a surplus of semi-fast stock but a shortage of suburban units. This deficiency was remedied by the downrating of 6001-21/4-44 to second class only, reclassification as 2SAP and renumbering as 5901-42 for use on Waterloo-Windsor and Weybridge services. Units 6022/3 escaped this fate because they were already involved in the still-continuing Wedgelock coupler trials. Because they retain their express gear ratio motors, the units are popular with motormen, although some journeys can be decidedly lively for passengers! The erstwhile 6015, now 2SAP 5915, hurries another of the same type over North Sheen crossing *(below)* on a Windsor-Waterloo working on 12 October 1974.
/R. W. Easterby; Alan Williams; J. Scrace; K. Lane

The most recent development on the suburban stock front has been the introduction in 1971 of the first of three prototype units for evaluation and development with a view to eventual series production to replace the ageing 4SUB units as well as adoption as the BR standard suburban unit. Two four-car (4PEP) units Nos 4001/2 were built, as well as a two-car (2PEP) unit No 2001 early in 1972, the latter principally to enable the formation of a ten car train for trial purposes on the Eastern Section.

The new units represent an almost total departure from previous Southern suburban practice; the bodies are of open, rapid transit-style construction with air-operated sliding doors and longitudinal as well as transverse seating. They have wide gangways between cars within each unit to allow ample circulation of passengers under crush conditions, and a centre door in the drivers cab for emergency access to adjacent units. There are no buffers, even at the outer ends, and a Scharfenberg automatic coupling which includes all brake and control line circuits has been provided, thus finally dispensing with the need for cumbersome jumper cables and making for a remarkably clean front end. All axles are motored, and on the four-car units there are additional shoebeams at the inner ends of the centre non-driving vehicles. Braking is electro-rheostatic as well as electro-pneumatic on disc brakes. There is no separate guard's compartment as such, and the guard travels in the rear, unoccupied driver's cab. There are only two types of vehicle—driving motor coaches and intermediate non-driving motor coaches.

As built, the units were fully air-conditioned, with no opening windows whatsoever, but it soon became obvious that this was unsatisfactory, and sliding 'airstream' type windows were fitted before they entered public service, the air conditioning equipment being retained for force-ventilation. Various types of internal decor and finish have been tried in the units, and the two-car unit 2001 was finished in unpainted aluminium, with red BR symbol and lettering, as well as a simplified form of bogie. One unpainted driving motor coach of 2001 was swapped with that of 4001 in 1973, and as unit 2001 subsequently disappeared into works (to re-appear on the Eastern Region as 920 001, a three-car 750V/25kV prototype for the Class 313 units) just one odd unpainted vehicle remains in use in the otherwise orthodox-blue 4001.

After extensive trials on the Western Section, the units were put into traffic on the Waterloo-Hampton Court and Shepperton branches, and apart from a month-long trial on the Eastern Section lines out of Charing Cross and Cannon Street—where they were not particularly well-received—they have remained on the Western Section ever since. There has been some criticism of the door and seating arrangements, and as a result of these tests, it seems likely that the two-door bodyshell with orthodox transverse

seating of the GN Class 313 units will be adopted for new construction, together with the 313's more upright, but otherwise similar, front end. Despite these criticisms—and that, after all, is what prototypes are built for—there can be no doubt that the PEP represents one of the largest single steps forward the Southern has ever made, especially in suburban stock design, although it is fair to say that it does not appear quite so progressive when compared with the LMS Wirral and Southport stock of 1938/9, or the LNER Shenfield stock of 1949. Such has been the conservatism of Southern thinking since the War! No production units have yet been ordered, but the advancing years of the bulk of the 4SUB and SR 4EPB units is such that a large-scale replacement programme during the late 1970s and early 1980s seems inevitable. Although as built the prototype units have a centre door and smaller, less vandal-prone windows, the similarity between the front end of the original mock up *(above left)* and that of 4001 *(below left)* on clearance tests in the Windsor line platforms at Waterloo on 4 July 1972 is obvious. The half-blue, half-silver nature of units 2001 and 4001 after the transposition of one of their driving motor coaches (and the fitting of sliding ventilators) is evident *(above)* as both units pass Raynes Park on the 13.14 Waterloo-Basingstoke special working on 10 October 1973. Adding a suitably modernistic flavour to the concrete environs of Tolworth *(below)* is 4001 on a Waterloo-Chessington working in August 1975.
/BR; R. E. Ruffell; J. Scrace; J. G. Glover

Extension of electrification to most of the remaining lines in Kent, heralded in the Modernisation Plan in January 1955, meant a vast new requirement for main-line stock, the first for almost two decades. So in summer, 1956 Eastleigh turned out six prototype units, two four-car buffet units (4BEP) Nos 7001/2 and four four-car corridor units (4CEP) Nos 7101-4.

Although built on BR Standard jigs, the units were essentially updated versions of the pre-War 4BUF and 4COR units. The motor coaches had a small brake van and a seven-bay saloon, flanked at each end by transverse vestibules with the doors; the poor loading/unloading characteristics of the 4COR motor coaches had clearly been noted, for an additional door was provided on each side, let direct into the centre bay. Both the trailer composite and trailer second were side-corridor vehicles identical in design to their BR Standard locomotive-hauled equivalents. The front end, too, was unremarkable *(left)*, being quite literally just an ordinary coach end fitted with windows and the necessary jumper cables; the BR Standard Pullman-type gangway was fitted, together with buckeye couplings, and the control gear was identical to the '1951 stock' suburban EPB units, with which the new units could work. . . Revised gearing arrangements, however, gave the units a maximum speed of 90mph—all previous units had a nominal maximum of 75mph—but it should be remarked

that it was several years before the full potential of this extra capability could be exploited—officially, at least! The one departure from 4COR practice was the return of the roller blind headcode panel to a rather clumsy, slightly off-centre position in the centre of the gangway, allowing the fitting of a second cab window on the offside.
The six prototype units went into service on the Brighton line (Nos 7001/2 as three-car units until the delivery of their buffet cars in early 1957) and have remained allocated there ever since, although they have made one or two brief sorties elsewhere from time to time. In recent years, they have monopolised the Mid-Sussex line services; 7104 rounds the sharp curve at Mitcham Junction at respectful pace (*below* on 1 August 1970 on a mid-day Victoria-Portsmouth/Bognor via Horsham working.
The Southern were evidently well-pleased with the prototypes, for the first batch of production units for the Thanet line electrification, 4BEPs 7003-12 and 4CEPs 7105-53, built in 1958/9, were virtually identical, save for the fitting of the later '1957 stock' camshaft control and the use of plastics rather than wood veneer for the interior decor, but one weakness to which the trials of the prototypes did not alert management was the quite appalling riding qualities that some units developed when out of shops for some time; it is no exaggeration to say that it was sometimes almost impossible to stand in the buffet cars when travelling at speed.
Assailed by complaining passengers, the Southern decided to equip the next batch of units, BEPs 7013-22 and CEPs 7154-7204, built in 1960/1 for Phase Two of the Kent Coast scheme, with Commonwealth-type roller-bearing fitted bogies on the trailers, as well as on the unmotored ends of the motor coaches. Similar bogies were also fitted retrospectively to the buffet cars of units 7001/3-12. Unit 7179 of the second batch pauses at Tonbridge *(below left)* in August 1962 on an afternoon Margate-Charing Cross working. */BR; P. R. Foster; Alan Williams*

Whereas the brake vans of the 4BEP and 4CEP units were quite adequate for normal use, they were quite incapable of dealing with the volume of luggage accompanying most boat train passengers. So, when Phase One of the Kent Coast scheme brought multiple-unit boat trains to Dover, the Southern provided two motor luggage vans—essentially BR full brakes on standard length underframes with full-width suburban-type standard front ends—to cope with this traffic. Each van is equipped with traction batteries to enable it to venture for short distances over unelectrified quayside lines, and a vacuum exhauster to enable non-powered freight vehicles to be towed. Eight more were provided for the Phase Two Scheme, which brought electric trains to Folkestone. No unit numbers were allocated, but in recent years the vans have carried their coach Nos 68001-10 on each end for ease of identification; 68010 heads a down boat train on 26 August 1975 *(above)* as it eases cautiously down the steep incline from Folkestone Junction into Folkestone Harbour station.

When, in 1964, the all-embracing Southern green livery, traditional on dc electric stock for just 50 years, gave way to BR rail blue, the Southern decided for the sake of uniformity to paint all its stock blue, even the express units, rather than the more usual blue-and-grey associated with Inter-City express stock. After a while, it became obvious that the blue was not wearing well, and in 1967 it was decided to paint the post-war express stock (but not the 4CORs) in the two tone livery, and it is in this present and decidedly more attractive blue and grey livery that Phase one 4CEP 7145 *(below left)* approaches Faversham on the 14.14 Dover Marine-Victoria on 31 May 1975, passing on the way Class 71 electric locomotive No 71 003, stabled at the platform end for the weekend.

In recent years, catering facilities on Kent Coast Services have been rationalised and reduced, and BEPs 7003-9 are now allocated to the Central Section, where they displaced pre-war stock. But the later units are still very much in evidence on Eastern section duties; 7020 speeds westward along the Channel coast near Abbotscliffe tunnel *(right)* on 8 July 1971 at the head of a Dover-Charing Cross working.

Nowadays, almost 20 years after they were introduced, the very-much BR Mk 1 4CEPs are decidedly inferior to the air-conditioned Mark 3 stock used on Inter-City services on other Regions. Yet the economics of the Southern's Inter-City lines are such, we are told (though some may find it difficult to believe when one compares loadings with other Regions) that replacement with more modern stock is out of the question 'before the end of the century'. In the interim therefore, it has been decided to refurbish the 4CEPs within their existing bodyshells, and in November 1975 Eastleigh turned out a prototype rebuild of unit 7153 *(below)* for trial and evaluation, and to establish the cost of modernising the entire 4BEP/4CEP fleet. The small guards/luggage vans in each motor coach, which were restrictive because of the number of access doors and the lack of a security cage, have been replaced by an additional eight-seat open bay and a transverse gangway giving access to the drivers cab. Instead, a single, larger guards/luggage compartment has been provided by converting two of the three second-class compartments in the trailer composite; the trailer corridor second has been completely gutted and converted to an open second. Seating and interior furnishing is generally to latest Mk 3 designs, and strip lighting is fitted in all the open coaches. The troublesome original bogies have been replaced with refurbished Commonwealth-type bogies salvaged from withdrawn locomotive-hauled stock, and for the first time on SR main-line stock much-needed public address equipment has been installed. */A. W. Hobson; J. H. Cooper-Smith (2); C. Long*

If the 4BEPs and 4CEPs can be excused their obsolescence on the grounds of age, their successors, the 4BIGs and 4CIGs, most certainly cannot. Introduced between 1964-6 to replace the 6PULs and 6PANs on the Brighton line, the 18 buffet car (4BIG) units Nos 7031-48 and 36 corridor (4CIG) units Nos 7301-36 were the first to be built away from Eastleigh since before the War, and broke with previous tradition by having a single large non-driving motor brake vehicle with all axles powered in the centre of the unit, instead of separate motor coaches at each end. The glass fibre front ends, with recessed panels for the control and brake jumper cables, were rounded at the top to meet the roof, but otherwise the units were uninspiring, their accommodation representing no material advance on that in the earlier 4CEPs, although their B5 bogies gave a better ride. The internal arrangements smacked of 'design by committee' and by the time the later batches were built—Nos 7049-58 and 7337-66 in 1970 to replace the 4CORs and 4BUFs on the Portsmouth line and Nos 7367-7438 in 1971/2 to replace the remaining 4CORs on the Reading and South Coast lines—the basically modified Mark 1 design looked decidedly obsolete alongside the first Mark 3 air-conditioned vehicles then being built. If the earlier 4CEP stock is expected to last into the 1990s, Southern travellers must presumably wait until the 21st Century to enjoy the air-conditioned comfort at present lavished on their companions north of the Thames.

The Brighton line units, of which batch 7315 *(above right)* brings up the rear of a Brighton-Victoria train near Scaynes Hill on 8 April 1966, were among the last to appear in green livery. They next appeared in blue, but by 1970 all were in blue and grey. One of the original batch leads two 4CEPs through Battersea Park and across the viaducts above Battersea Wharf *(right)* as it approaches journeys end with the 13.30 Hastings-Eastbourne-Victoria on 22 May of that year.

Although built for the Portsmouth line, the later batches of 4CIGs and 4BIGs based on the South Western Division are not infrequent performers on the Bournemouth line, although they are hard pressed to maintain the timings of the more-powerful 4REPs normally used on that route. When the Bournemouth line expresess were stepped up to an hourly interval in 1974, there was a temporary shortage of stock owing to late delivery of additional units; standing in for a 4REP that summer are 4BIG No 7053 and two 4CIGs approaching Surbiton *(above)* at speed on an up morning peak hour semi-fast. */John Vaughan; Colin Gifford; Alan Williams;*

Described by a less-than impressed railwayman as a '4SUB with corridors', the 4VEPs, first introduced in 1967 for semi-fast services on the newly-electrified Bournemouth lines, were like the almost contemporary CIGs, a compromise based on an outdated design. They are 'jack-of-all-trades' units and therefore, predictably, masters of none. Their '3+2' high density seating, with doors to each bay, is ideal for commuter use, but the cramped seating is less-well received when the units are used, often indiscriminately, on express workings with 4CEPs and 4CIGs, with which they can interwork. The front ends are identical to those used on the 4CIGs, and the 250hp motors combine rapid acceleration with a maximum speed of 90mph. Despite their rather austere nature, somewhat relieved externally since the adoption (although quite unjustified) of blue and grey Inter-City livery, the Southern clearly sees them as the standard semi-fast/outer suburban unit for the next few decades, and examples of this now most numerous class can be found almost anywhere on the system.

The first 20 VEPs, Nos 7701-20, were allocated to Bournemouth in readiness for the commencement of full public electric working in July 1967 and, because they are the only units of the class with AWS equipment, they have remained on Bournemouth line services ever since. Newly-delivered 7708 accelerates away beneath the twin footbridges south of Woking *(right)* on a trial trip to Basingstoke in the spring of 1967. A further 95 units, Nos 7720-7815, were built between 1967 and 1970 to replace first the 4LAVs on the Brighton line, and then the bulk of the 2BILs and 2HALs on South Western and Central Division London-South Coast workings. In 1972, a further batch, Nos 7816-53, appeared to finally displace the remaining 2BILs, 2HALs and some 4CORs, and in 1973 delivery of the latest batch, Nos 7854-94 began, these

later units going to the Eastern section where they displaced some SR and BR 2HAPs which, after conversion to second class only, have in turn, by a cascade process, displaced older 4SUB units. One of the latest units, 7868, brakes for picturesque Kearsney *(above left)* on the 10.10 Victoria-Dover Priory stopping train on 25 August 1975.

Units 7739/41/2 were not put into traffic as such when they were delivered in 1968; instead, because of the dire shortage of express stock suitable for use on the Bournemouth line, they were formed into one five-car and one three-car unit, both numbered 8001 and collectively classified 8VAB. The theory was that the five-car unit, formed of two driving trailers, two motor coaches and a rewired, ex-locomotive-hauled kitchen-buffet, would act as the main tractor unit, while the three-car unit, formed of a motor coach sandwiched between two driving trailers, would provide the additional power to propel a 4TC unit. One of the motor coaches in the five-car unit had its doors premanently locked and, despite its nominal 3+2 seating, was equipped with tables and used for the service of meals on a 2+1 basis. The three motor coaches gave the 8VAB a total of 3,300hp, and when operating as an eight-car unit without an accompanying trailer unit, could be relied upon for some lively running! On one such occasion, 8001 pauses briefly at Woking *(below right)* on a winter Sunday Bournemouth-Waterloo working in late 1969; note the small aluminium British Rail symbol beneath the cab window, originally carried by all the earlier 4VEPs, as well as by the Bournemouth line express stock. The unique 8001 'twins' were reformed into conventional 4VEPs when additional 4REPs were delivered in 1974. */A W Hobson; Alan Williams (2)*

Like the 4BIGs and 4CIGs, the new stock provided for the Bournemouth line electrification in 1967 has come in for much criticism on the grounds of being obsolescent when new. But new is a word which has to be applied with some caution in connection with this stock, for the majority of vehicles are merely rebuilt or refurbished Mark 1 vehicles, some dating from the 1950s, fitted with new B5 bogies.

The operating requirements of the Bournemouth line scheme were unique; in addition to a need for locomotives for boat train and freight traffic, there was the need for part of a Waterloo-Bournemouth train to continue on over unelectrified metals to Weymouth. Short of providing locomotive-hauled trains throughout with a change of locomotive at the Bournemouth extremity of the conductor rail, this was an entirely new requirement for multiple-unit stock.

It was met by a novel 'tractor-and-trailer' unit concept; 11 four-car (4REP) tractor units, Nos 3001-11, were provided, to work with 28 four-car trailer (4TC) and three three-car trailer (3TC) units, Nos 401-28 and 301-3 respectively. The tractor units consisted of two new eight-bay motor open seconds flanking a refurbished ex-steam stock trailer buffet and a trailer brake first converted from a standard corridor composite, the new brake van taking the place of the second-class seats. Both bogies of both motor coaches were powered, each axle carrying a 365hp traction motor and giving an unprecedented 2,920hp in a single four-car unit. The 4TC trailer units consisted of two driving trailer open seconds, identical in layout to the motor seconds of the 4REPs, flanking a trailer first and trailer brake second. The 3TC units were the same but omitted the trailer first and were thus second class only. All the vehicles in these units were rebuilt or refurbished steam stock, the driving trailer open seconds being open seconds with a drivers cab in place of the original end lavatories! The same glass-fibre front end as the 4CIGs and 4VEPs is employed and the maximum speed is 90mph. Each 4REP normally works coupled to two 4TC units, one of which is detached at Bournemouth and proceeds to Weymouth diesel locomotive-hauled. On the return trip, it is propelled by the diesel locomotove, allowing it to be coupled directly to the rear of an up 4REP/4TC formation waiting at Bournemouth for the return trip to Waterloo. The 4REPs have proved themselves to be lively runners, speeds well in excess of 100mph having been attained on test. When, as sometimes happens, they work coupled to only one 4TC as an eight-car train, acceleration can be phenomenal! In normal circumstances they rarely work alone, and although they are electrically compatible with and can therefore in theory work coupled to other post-war express stock, they are in practice normally forbidden to do so because the high initial current consumption on starting of any such combination would trip most circuit breakers.

Increasing traffic on the Bournemouth line persuaded the Southern to increase the frequency of the two-hourly Waterloo-Southampton-Bournemouth expresses to hourly in 1974, and for this purpose and to replace the temporary 8VAB No 8001, four more 4REPs, Nos 3012-5 were built, again with new motor coaches and salvaged trailers, and amazingly still to the original Mark 1 outline, being identical to their predecessors. These eight motor coaches must be among the last Mark 1 vehicles to be built, and are an indictment of the Southern's short-sighted, conservative post-War rolling stock policy. At the same time, the three 3TC units 301-3 were given a refurbished trailer first and became 4TCs 429-431, and three more complete conversions, Nos 432-4, were turned out from York.

In addition to working with the 4REP units, the 4TC units can be hauled—and propelled—by Class 73 and 74 electro-diesels, as well as the Birmingham Class 33/1 diesel-electrics. Not long out of works and wearing the original all-blue livery, 4TC No 414 heads through then-still semaphore Byfleet & New Haw *(above left)*, propelled by Class 73 electro-diesel No E6012 on a test run on 13 February 1967, prior to the introduction of some electric workings to Bournemouth in steam timings the following month. Delivery of the 4REPs was later than the 4TCs, and steam traction survived on some Bournemouth services until the eve of the introduction of the full electric timetable. With the distinctive whine of its powerful motors filling the air, 4REP 3003 leaves St Johns cutting *(below left)* and approaches Woking Junction at speed on an up test run on an April Saturday in 1967.

Because of the need to ensure that at least one 4TC unit is provided at the country end, to form the diesel-powered Bournemouth-Weymouth portion, Waterloo-Bournemouth expresses are almost invariably formed with the powered 4REP unit at the London end—meaning a walk the length of the 12-car train for a Weymouth passenger seeking a meal or a snack! Swinging through the curves at Vauxhall on an up afternoon Bournemouth-Waterloo semi-fast on 4 November 1975 is 4REP 3009 *(next page)*, overtaking as it does so 4EPB 5117 restarting on an up Chessington working. */J. H. Bird; Alan Williams; F. R. Kerr*

5117
18

3009
92

In contrast to the urgency and enthusiasm with which it electrified its passenger services, the Southern did nothing to switch its then still considerable freight traffic over to electric traction. This was partly due to the need to keep some quite modern steam motive power, displaced from passenger work, usefully employed, but mainly because of the safety problems of third-rail electrification in marshalling yards and, more important still, the need to perfect a design which could 'coast' across the many gaps in the conductor rails at busy junctions without 'snatching' on the couplings. Nevertheless, the Southern was acutely aware that the full benefits of electrification could only be realised if all traffic was electrically worked and construction of two prototype Co-Co locomotives to Raworth's design was well advanced when War broke out. Because they promised to bring savings in labour and fuel, it was decided to press on with construction as time and materials permitted, and the first, CC1, was turned out in 1941. With a huge, deep frame and an angular, welded front end and domed cab roof which clearly owed allegiance to the 1939 2HALs, the newcomer looked a robust design; it quickly proved its worth by handling 750 ton passenger and 1,000 ton freight trains with apparent ease.

To overcome the 'gapping' problem, Raworth had devised a booster system whereby, instead of supplying current direct to the six 245hp pressure-ventilated motors, the line voltage drove a motor-generator set, which, because it was fitted with a large flywheel, would continue to run on,

76

generating current, while the locomotive traversed even the longest rail gaps. For work in marshalling yards, it was decided that conductor rail was simply too dangerous, particularly under wartime conditions; it was proposed to erect low voltage, tramway-type overhead instead, and each locomotive was fitted with a pantograph.

The second locomotive, CC2, appeared in 1943; it was identical to its predecessor, and was put to work on similar duties. On Nationalisation in 1948, CC1 and CC2 became 20001/2 under the British Railways numbering scheme, and a third locomotive, 20003, was added to stock later that year. Slightly heavier and longer than its predecessors, 20003 had flat, 4SUB-like front ends.

When first built, CC1 was equipped with a standard SR headcode panel for stencil letters. But as no appropriate headcodes existed, combined headlamp/disc units were soon added, so that the standard SR steam disc headcode could be displayed, as on CC1 *(above left)* trundling east through Chichester with a mixed freight in the last months of 1947 before Nationalisation. In practice, the headcode panel was hardly used at all; 20003, with discs only, sets out *(below left)* from Victoria for Newhaven on 15 May 1949 with the first electrically-worked boat train, made possible by the electrification of the harbour lines two years previously.

Like its two predecessors, 20003 was originally painted Southern green; in 1950 the three locomotives were painted black, with broad white horizontal lining. By the early 1960s they had all acquired the much more pleasing lined BR locomotive green livery, and like everything else, succumbed to BR rail blue later in the same decade.

With the demise of steam, and the arrival of BR design diesel and electric locomotives, discs disappeared and a whole new series of headcodes, including letters as well as numbers, were introduced; Nos 20001-3 were fitted with roller-blind headcode panels, and with the resultant much cleaner front end, 20001 emerges from the castellated north portal of Clayton Tunnel *(right)* with an up afternoon van train in January 1969, just a few weeks before the withdrawal of all three locomotives. */SR (2); John H Bird*

The Kent Coast electrification schemes, unlike the pre-war Southern extensions, envisaged the total elimination of steam traction, even from freight, parcels and special trains. To work this traffic, and boat trains which could not be covered by multiple-units, such as the 'Golden Arrow' and 'Night Ferry', 14 Bo-Bo electric locomotives, Nos E5000-13, were built at Doncaster in 1959, and a further 10, Nos E5014-23, in 1960. They had the same motor generator booster system as the earlier Southern Railway Co-Co locomotives, but were lighter, with spring-borne motors and flexible drives rather than the usual axle-hung nose-suspended arrangement. Short shoebeams were fitted to each axle, and all locomotives were fitted with pantographs to work on the tramway-type overhead erected in several marshalling yards, including the Hither Green complex from which the erstwhile E5011, now Class 71 No 71 011, is departing *(back cover)* with a freight from the Eastern Region to Chatham on 25 February 1976.

Now but a memory, the 'Golden Arrow' was for a decade the sole preserve of the Class 71s, from the introduction of electric working until the withdrawal of the Pullman cars and replacement with orthodox multiple-units. Suitably bedecked with miniature versions of the Union Jack and the Tricolour, as well as the specially-made headboard, E5019 (now converted to an electro-diesel) rests at Dover Marine *(below left)* after arrival with the down summer all-Pullman train in June 1964.

Whilst the Class 71s were useful machines, careful diagramming was necessary to ensure that they worked only into yards where conductor rail or overhead was available, and even then, they often had to rely on diesel shunters. And at night or weekends, when power supplies were interrupted for maintenance work, they would often have to be sent on long detours simply to stay 'on the juice'. So in 1962, the Southern Engineers came up with a box of tricks it dubbed an 'electro-diesel'. Although uninspiring externally—their box-like bodies are narrow and flat-sided to allow them to go anywhere without restriction—the six prototypes, Nos E6001-6, soon proved that they were equal to the engineers claim that they could do anything anywhere. Fitted with four 400hp traction motors, retractable shoegear and a 600bhp diesel engine similar to that fitted to the Hastings and Hampshire diesel-electric units, these remarkable machines can work either as straight electric locomotives, or as diesels if no

power supply is available. Fitted with buck-eye couplings, they can work in multiple with all EP stock, suburban as well as main line, with all the various types of Southern diesel-electric unit, with the Class 74 electro-diesels and the Class 33 diesel electric locomotives, as well as simply hauling air or vacuum-braked passenger or freight stock! Needless to say, their superiority in operating terms over straight electric locomotives soon became apparent, and in 1967 43 more locomotives, Nos E6007-49, were provided for the Bournemouth electrification, where in addition to all their other talents, they happily propel the TC trailer units (see page 85). The first six locomotives are now Class 73/0 Nos 73 001-6, and the later batch Class 73/1 Nos 73 101-42, one, No E6027 having been written off as a result of accident damage. With its retractable shoegear clearly visible *(below)*, 73 116 eases a train of empty coal wagons off the up slow lines and onto the West London line just south of Clapham Junction on September 18 1974. The newest additions to the SR electric locomotive fleet are, in good Southern tradition, not new at all! Reorganisation of Eastern Section services in the mid-1960s, and particularly the decline in locomotive-hauled trains, had rendered some of the Class 71 locomotives surplus to requirements. So, encouraged by the success of the 'baby' electro-diesels, the Southern converted 10, Nos E5003/5/6/15-7/9/21/3/4, to Class 74 electro-diesels Nos E6101-10, now 74 001-10. They retained their original spring-borne traction motors and booster set, but the pantograph was removed and a 650bhp diesel engine fitted, as well as buck-eye couplings and air and control jumper cables to give the same versatility as their smaller Class 73 sisters, with which they can work in multiple. Although in theory considerably more powerful than the Class 73s, Nos 74 001-10 have been dogged by failures, mainly of their sophisticated electronic control system, and the smaller locomotives have deputised for them with apparent ease. However, the 74s find regular employment on Southampton and Weymouth boat trains; running on its diesel engine 74 003 winds the empty stock of an up boat train back from Waterloo beneath Clapham C Box *(next page)* and into Clapham Yard on 18 September 1974. */Alan Williams; B Morrison (3)*